AI Freelancing 101: Your First Step to Six Figures

A Beginner's Blueprint to Earning Big with Artificial Intelligence

By

Ernie Braveboy

Unlock the Potential of AI Conversations: Discover "ChatGPT Mastery – Your First Prompt Unlocked

ChatGPT
MASTERY
YOUR FIRST PROMPT
UNLOCKED
A Beginner's Guide to Crafting
Perfect Prompts and
Mastering ChatGPT
ERNIE BRAVEBOY

Table of Contents

Foreword

In an era where the digital landscape is perpetually evolving, the emergence of artificial intelligence (AI) as a pivotal force in reshaping industries is undeniable. Amidst this technological revolution, the freelancing world has witnessed a transformative shift, opening up a realm of opportunities for those ready to harness the power of AI. "AI Freelancing 101: Your First Step to Six Figures," authored by Ernie Braveboy, is more than just a book; it is a gateway to understanding and leveraging these opportunities to not just survive but thrive in the competitive freelancing market.

Ernie Braveboy, with his insightful and forward-thinking approach, has crafted a guide that is both a beacon for beginners and a reference point for seasoned freelancers. This book demystifies the complex world of AI, making it accessible and actionable for individuals who aspire to elevate their freelancing careers to unprecedented heights.

What sets this book apart is not just its comprehensive coverage of AI tools and techniques, but its deep understanding of the freelance economy's nuances. From identifying in-demand AI skills to navigating the intricacies of client relationships, "AI Freelancing 101" offers a holistic view of what it takes to succeed.

As we stand on the brink of a new digital dawn, the fusion of AI and freelancing presents a unique blend of challenges and rewards. Ernie doesn't shy away from discussing the hurdles;

instead, he offers practical solutions, drawing from real-life examples and success stories that inspire and instruct.

Whether you are taking your first step into freelancing or looking to infuse AI into your freelance endeavors, this book is your compass. It not only equips you with the knowledge to make informed decisions but also empowers you to take bold steps towards achieving your financial goals.

As you turn the pages of "AI Freelancing 101", remember that the journey to a six-figure income is not a sprint but a marathon. With Ernie Braveboy's guidance, you are not just preparing for the future of work; you are actively shaping it.

Welcome to the future of freelancing.

Acknowledgments

The creation of "AI Freelancing 101: Your First Step to Six Figures" has been an incredible journey, one enriched and made possible by the support and encouragement of many.

To my family, whose unwavering support and love have been my foundation, I am eternally grateful. Your belief in my work has been the light guiding me through the countless hours spent bringing this book to life.

I owe a debt of gratitude to my peers and mentors in the AI and freelancing fields. Your invaluable insights and shared experiences have not only shaped this book but have also deeply influenced my perspective on the transformative power of AI in freelancing.

My heartfelt thanks go to my editor, whose meticulous attention to detail and dedication to excellence have been instrumental in refining my thoughts into the coherent narrative presented in this book.

To the brave freelancers who opened up about their journeys, thank you for your honesty and willingness to share. Your stories are the heartbeat of this guide, offering readers a glimpse into the real-world application of the strategies discussed.

I am also grateful to the AI research community for their relentless pursuit of innovation. The technologies you've developed are the bedrock upon which this book stands, heralding a new era for freelancers everywhere.

And finally, to you, the reader, for choosing to embark on this journey with me. Your commitment to exploring new frontiers in work and technology is the ultimate inspiration behind this book. Together, we venture into a promising future where AI is not just a tool, but a partner in crafting a successful freelance career.

Thank you all for being pillars of support and sources of inspiration throughout this endeavor.

Ernie Braveboy

Introduction

Welcome to "AI Freelancing 101: Your First Step to Six Figures," a guide designed to usher you into the new era of work where artificial intelligence meets freelancing. If you're holding this book, you're likely standing at the crossroads of curiosity and ambition, pondering how the digital revolution can pave the way for your financial success. You're in the right place.

The fusion of AI and freelancing is more than just a trend; it's a transformative shift in how work is done, valued, and compensated. This book is born out of a vision to demystify AI for those who are not tech wizards but are eager to learn and leverage this burgeoning technology to create a thriving freelance career.

The journey into AI freelancing is not about turning you into a machine learning expert overnight. Instead, it's about equipping you with the knowledge and tools to harness AI's power, enhance your skills, and open up new avenues for income that were previously unimaginable.

As we venture through these pages, we'll explore what AI really means in the context of freelancing. You'll discover how AI can streamline tasks, unearth opportunities, and elevate the quality of work you offer. From content creation and design to data analysis and beyond, AI's applications are vast and varied.

But this book is more than just an exploration of AI's potential; it's a practical guide to applying these insights to your freelance career. You'll learn how to identify AI tools that can give you a competitive edge, develop skills in high demand, and position yourself in the market to attract lucrative projects.

Perhaps you're wondering if AI is too complex, too technical, or too futuristic for your current skill set. Let me assure you, the AI revolution in freelancing is for everyone willing to learn, adapt, and grow. This book is your first step towards understanding how you fit into this new landscape, regardless of your background.

"AI Freelancing 101" is not just about surviving in a competitive market; it's about thriving, innovating, and reaching financial heights you've only dreamed of. So, let's embark on this journey together, with an open mind and the resolve to embrace the future of freelancing, where AI is not just an advantage but a necessity for success.

Welcome to your future.

Ernie Braveboy

The Rise of AI and Freelancing

In the last decade, two significant trends have reshaped the landscape of work and opportunity: the astonishing rise of Artificial Intelligence (AI) and the robust growth of the freelancing economy. Individually, each has made profound impacts, but together, they are forging a new frontier for professionals around the world.

The AI Revolution

AI's journey from a niche scientific discipline to a cornerstone of modern technological advancement is nothing short of remarkable. Today, AI is not just a buzzword but a tangible force driving innovation across sectors—from healthcare and education to finance and entertainment. Its capabilities, from understanding human language with natural language processing to recognizing patterns and improving decision-making with machine learning, have opened up new vistas for efficiency, creativity, and problem-solving.

But AI's rise is not just about sophisticated algorithms and futuristic robots; it's about how these technologies can augment human potential. For freelancers, AI tools offer the promise of automating mundane tasks, providing insightful data analysis, and enhancing creative outputs in ways previously unimaginable.

The Freelancing Surge

Parallel to the AI boom, freelancing has emerged from the shadows of the gig economy to become a dominant mode of employment. Fueled by digital platforms, a shift towards remote work, and a growing desire for work-life balance, more individuals are choosing the freelance path. This shift is not merely about the freedom to choose projects or set one's schedule; it's a reflection of a deeper change in how work is valued, delivered, and managed.

Today, freelancers contribute significantly to the global economy, offering a wide array of services, from writing and graphic design to software development and digital marketing. The flexibility and scalability of freelancing have made it an attractive option for many, especially in an era where traditional job security can no longer be taken for granted.

Convergence of AI and Freelancing

The convergence of AI and freelancing is a natural progression in this evolving work environment. AI tools empower freelancers to deliver more value, work more efficiently, and stand out in a crowded market. Whether it's leveraging AI for creative design, utilizing machine learning algorithms for market analysis, or employing AI-powered platforms for project management, the integration of AI into freelancing is creating unparalleled opportunities for those ready to embrace it.

This convergence also addresses some of the fundamental challenges of freelancing, such as time management, client acquisition, and maintaining a steady income. With AI, freelancers can automate repetitive tasks, gain insights into market trends, and tailor their services to meet the specific needs of their clients more effectively.

Looking Ahead

As we stand at the cusp of this new era, the potential for AI-driven freelancing is boundless. However, navigating this landscape requires more than just an understanding of AI technologies; it demands a mindset shift towards continuous learning, adaptability, and innovation.

In the chapters that follow, we'll delve deeper into how you can harness the power of AI to transform your freelancing career. From identifying the right AI tools to integrating them into your workflow and scaling your freelance business, this book is your guide to thriving in the age of AI and freelancing.

Welcome to the future of work. The journey begins now.

Chapter 1: Understanding AI

The Dawn of Artificial Intelligence

Artificial Intelligence (AI) is a field of computer science dedicated to creating systems capable of performing tasks that typically require human intelligence. These tasks include learning, decision-making, problem-solving, and more. The inception of AI traces back to the mid-20th century when the dream of creating intelligent machines began to take shape. Today, AI is not just a reality but a pivotal force driving innovation across industries.

The Many Faces of AI

AI can be broadly categorized into two types: Narrow AI and General AI. Narrow AI, also known as Weak AI, focuses on executing a specific task with intelligence, such as facial recognition or internet searches. In contrast, General AI, or Strong AI, encompasses systems that can understand, learn, and apply intelligence across a broad range of tasks, akin to human cognitive abilities. As of now, General AI remains largely theoretical, while Narrow AI is what we interact with in our daily lives through various applications and services.

How AI Works

At the heart of AI are algorithms, which are sets of rules or instructions that guide the AI system in analyzing data, making decisions, and learning from outcomes. Machine Learning (ML), a subset of AI, enables systems to learn and improve from experience without being explicitly programmed for each specific task. Another exciting area within AI is Deep Learning, which involves neural networks with many layers, mimicking the human brain's structure and function to process data in complex ways.

AI in Our Daily Lives

AI's integration into our daily lives is so seamless that we often take its presence for granted. From personalized recommendations on streaming services and online shopping to voice assistants like Siri and Alexa, AI enhances our experiences and efficiency. In the workplace, AI applications range from customer service chatbots and automated email sorting to sophisticated data analysis and predictive modeling.

The Impact of AI on Freelancing

For freelancers, AI opens up a new realm of possibilities. It offers tools for enhancing productivity, creativity, and service quality. AI can automate routine tasks, allowing freelancers to focus on high-value activities. It also provides insights into market trends and client behaviors, enabling freelancers to tailor their offerings more effectively. Moreover, AI-powered platforms can connect freelancers with clients, streamline project management, and facilitate smoother communication and collaboration.

Embracing AI as a Freelancer

To harness AI's potential, freelancers must first develop a foundational understanding of AI technologies and their applications. This doesn't necessarily mean becoming an AI expert but rather gaining sufficient knowledge to utilize AI tools and services effectively. Staying updated with AI trends and continuously exploring new tools can significantly enhance a freelancer's competitiveness and efficiency.

Conclusion

Understanding AI is the first step towards unlocking its potential in the freelancing world. As AI continues to evolve, its impact on freelancing will only grow, making it an indispensable tool for those looking to thrive in the digital economy. The subsequent chapters will delve deeper into specific AI applications and how freelancers can leverage these technologies to elevate their careers.

1.1 What is Artificial Intelligence?

Artificial Intelligence (AI) is a transformative branch of computer science that aims to create systems capable of performing tasks that would typically require human intelligence. These tasks encompass a wide range, including understanding natural language, recognizing patterns and images, making decisions, solving complex problems, and even learning from past experiences. At its core, AI seeks to mimic the cognitive functions of the human mind through a combination of data, algorithms, and computational power.

The Essence of AI

The essence of AI lies in its ability to process vast amounts of data quickly and efficiently, identifying patterns and insights that might elude human analysis. Unlike traditional computer programs that follow a strict set of rules, AI systems can adapt their responses based on the information they process. This adaptability is what sets AI apart, enabling it to tackle tasks of varying complexity and nuance.

AI's Building Blocks

AI is built on several foundational technologies:

- **Machine Learning (ML)**: This is the backbone of most AI systems today. ML enables computers to learn from and make decisions based on data, improving their accuracy over time without being explicitly programmed for each task.
- **Neural Networks**: Inspired by the human brain's structure, neural networks are a series of algorithms that capture the relationships between various underlying variables and process data in a layered, hierarchical manner.
- **Natural Language Processing (NLP)**: NLP allows computers to understand, interpret, and respond to human language in a way that is both meaningful and useful.
- **Robotics**: While not all AI involves robots, robotics often incorporates AI to enable autonomous movement and decision-making in machines.
- **Computer Vision**: This technology enables machines to interpret and make decisions based on visual data, mimicking human visual understanding.

The Scope of AI

AI's applications are incredibly diverse, touching nearly every aspect of our lives and work. From the algorithms that curate our social media feeds and recommend products online to more complex applications like autonomous vehicles and predictive healthcare diagnostics, AI's footprint is expanding rapidly.

For freelancers, AI presents a wealth of opportunities to streamline workflows, enhance service offerings, and tap into new markets. Whether it's through automating administrative tasks, providing advanced analytics services, or creating AI-driven content, understanding and leveraging AI can significantly elevate a freelancer's value proposition in the digital marketplace.

The Future of AI

As we look ahead, the potential of AI continues to unfold, promising even more sophisticated applications and tools. The ongoing advancements in AI research and development herald a future where AI's integration into our professional and personal lives becomes even more seamless and impactful.

Understanding AI is crucial for anyone looking to navigate the future of work, especially for freelancers aiming to stay competitive and innovative in a rapidly evolving digital economy. As we delve deeper into AI's applications in the following sections, it's important to keep in mind that AI is not just a technological tool but a catalyst for transformation across industries and professions.

1.2 The Impact of AI on Various Industries

The advent of Artificial Intelligence (AI) has ushered in a new era of innovation and efficiency across various sectors. By automating complex processes, providing deeper insights into data, and enhancing customer experiences, AI is not just transforming industries; it's redefining the very nature of work and service delivery. Here's how AI is impacting some key industries:

Healthcare

In healthcare, AI is revolutionizing patient care and research. From predictive analytics that forecast outbreaks and identify at-risk patients, to AI-driven diagnostics that can detect diseases with greater accuracy than ever before, AI is enhancing the efficiency and effectiveness of healthcare services. Moreover, AI-powered robots are assisting in surgeries, offering precision that complements the surgeons' expertise.

Finance

The finance industry has embraced AI for fraud detection, risk management, and personalized customer services. AI algorithms analyze transaction patterns to identify fraudulent activities in real-time, significantly reducing financial losses. In investment and wealth management, AI-driven platforms provide personalized advice and predictive market insights, democratizing access to financial expertise.

Retail and E-Commerce

AI is transforming the retail and e-commerce sector by personalizing the shopping experience. Through machine learning algorithms, companies can offer personalized product recommendations, optimize inventory management, and streamline logistics. Chatbots and virtual assistants enhance customer service by providing instant, 24/7 support.

Manufacturing

In manufacturing, AI is key to predictive maintenance, quality control, and supply chain optimization. By analyzing data from machinery, AI predicts when equipment might fail, reducing downtime and maintenance costs. Computer vision systems ensure quality control by identifying defects more accurately than the human eye, and AI-driven analytics optimize supply chain logistics, making manufacturing processes more efficient and cost-effective.

Entertainment and Media

AI is reshaping content creation and consumption in the entertainment and media industry. From algorithms that recommend movies and music based on user preferences to AI tools that assist in creating music, writing scripts, and even generating art, AI is enhancing creativity and personalizing user experiences.

Education

AI's impact on education is multifaceted, offering personalized learning experiences, automating administrative tasks, and providing tutors and students with tools that adapt to individual learning styles. AI-driven analytics help educators identify areas where students struggle, allowing for more targeted teaching approaches.

Transportation and Logistics

AI is at the forefront of autonomous vehicle technology, with self-driving cars and drones set to redefine mobility and logistics. In addition to improving safety and efficiency on the roads, AI optimizes routing and logistics operations, saving time and reducing costs for businesses and consumers alike.

Freelancing and the Gig Economy

For freelancers and gig workers, AI opens up new avenues for income and innovation. From AI-powered design tools that enhance creativity to analytics platforms that provide insights into market trends, freelancers can leverage AI to offer more competitive services. Moreover, AI-driven platforms are making it easier for freelancers to connect with potential clients, manage projects, and automate administrative tasks, allowing them to focus on higher-value work.

Conclusion

The impact of AI across these industries is just the beginning. As AI technology continues to evolve, its potential to drive further innovation and efficiency is boundless. For professionals, including freelancers, understanding and adapting to AI's advancements is crucial for staying relevant and competitive in this rapidly changing landscape. The next sections will delve into how freelancers, in particular, can harness AI to enhance their services and capitalize on the opportunities presented by this technological revolution.

1.3 AI Myths Debunked

As Artificial Intelligence (AI) becomes more integrated into our lives and industries, myths and misconceptions about its capabilities, intentions, and impacts have proliferated. These myths can create unnecessary fears, misunderstandings, and resistance to adopting AI technologies. Let's debunk some of the most common AI myths to clarify what AI can and cannot do.

Myth 1: AI Can Surpass Human Intelligence Imminently

Reality: The concept of AI surpassing human intelligence across all areas, known as Artificial General Intelligence (AGI), remains largely theoretical. Today's AI, or Narrow AI, excels at specific tasks but lacks the general reasoning and emotional understanding that characterize human intelligence. Achieving AGI is a complex challenge that researchers believe is still many years, if not decades, away.

Myth 2: AI Will Lead to Massive Job Displacement

Reality: While AI will undoubtedly transform certain jobs and industries, it's more about job evolution than wholesale displacement. Many tasks automated by AI are those that are repetitive and monotonous, allowing humans to focus on more creative, strategic, and interpersonal tasks. Moreover, AI is creating new job categories and industries, demanding new skills and roles that didn't exist before.

Myth 3: AI Operates Without Bias

Reality: AI systems learn from data, and if that data contains biases, the AI's decisions and predictions will likely reflect those biases. It's crucial to approach AI development and deployment with an awareness of potential biases and implement measures to minimize their impact. This includes diverse data sets and continuous monitoring for biased outcomes.

Myth 4: AI Can Make Autonomous Decisions and Actions

Reality: AI systems do not possess consciousness or independent desires. When AI "makes decisions," it's following a set of programmed algorithms and analyzing data within predefined parameters. Humans set these parameters and goals, and any autonomy is limited to the scope defined by human developers.

Myth 5: Implementing AI Requires Massive Resources and Expertise

Reality: While developing cutting-edge AI technologies may require significant resources, many AI tools and applications are designed to be accessible to non-experts. Cloud-based AI services and user-friendly platforms allow businesses and individuals, including freelancers, to leverage AI without the need for deep technical knowledge or substantial investments.

Myth 6: AI Is Only for Large Corporations and Tech Giants

Reality: AI technology is increasingly democratized, with tools and platforms available for businesses and individuals of all sizes. Freelancers and small businesses can utilize AI for various tasks, such as data analysis, content creation, and administrative automation, leveling the playing field with larger entities.

Conclusion

Debunking these myths is crucial for understanding AI's true potential and limitations. AI is a tool created by and for humans, designed to enhance our capabilities, not replace them. For freelancers, dispelling these myths opens up a world of possibilities for harnessing AI to improve efficiency, creativity, and service offerings, ensuring they remain competitive in a rapidly evolving digital landscape.

Chapter 2: The World of Freelancing

The landscape of work has undergone a seismic shift over the past decade, with freelancing emerging as a dominant force in the global economy. This chapter delves into the world of freelancing, exploring its rise, the opportunities it presents, and the challenges freelancers face in a digital-first era.

The Rise of Freelancing

Freelancing has evolved from being a side gig or a stopgap between jobs to a full-fledged career choice for millions worldwide. This shift is propelled by several factors, including the desire for work-life balance, the autonomy to choose projects that align with personal values and interests, and the opportunity to work remotely. Digital platforms have also played a crucial role, connecting freelancers with clients across the globe and creating a vibrant, dynamic marketplace for freelance work.

Opportunities in Freelancing

The freelance economy offers a plethora of opportunities across various sectors, from creative fields like writing, design, and multimedia to technical domains such as software development, data analysis, and digital marketing. The advent of AI and other emerging technologies has further expanded these opportunities, enabling freelancers to offer innovative services and solutions that leverage the power of AI.

Navigating the Freelance Landscape

While freelancing offers freedom and flexibility, it also comes with its own set of challenges. Freelancers must navigate the uncertainties of variable income, manage their own schedules and deadlines, and continuously market their services to maintain a steady stream of work. Additionally, freelancers need to stay abreast of industry trends and technological advancements to remain competitive.

The Role of AI in Freelancing

AI is transforming the freelance landscape in several ways. It's automating routine tasks, enabling freelancers to focus on higher-value work, and providing tools that enhance creativity and productivity. AI-driven platforms are also making it easier for freelancers to find work, connect with clients, and manage projects. Furthermore, AI is opening up new avenues for freelancers to specialize in, such as AI-driven analytics, content creation, and user experience design.

Building a Successful Freelance Career

To build a successful freelance career, one must go beyond mastering their craft. It involves developing a strong personal brand, building a professional network, effectively managing projects, and delivering consistent value to clients. Financial management, including setting competitive rates and planning for periods of variable income, is also crucial.

Conclusion

The world of freelancing is dynamic and full of potential. Embracing this mode of work requires adaptability, continuous learning, and a proactive approach to challenges. As AI continues to shape the future of work, freelancers who leverage these technologies can enhance their offerings, streamline their workflows, and position themselves at the forefront of their respective fields.

In the following chapters, we will explore how freelancers can specifically harness AI to elevate their freelance careers, focusing on practical applications, tools, and strategies for success in the AI-augmented freelance economy.

2.1 Why Choose Freelancing?

The allure of freelancing is more potent than ever, drawing individuals from diverse professional backgrounds into its fold. The decision to venture into freelancing is often driven by a blend of personal aspirations, lifestyle choices, and the desire for professional autonomy. Here are some compelling reasons why many are choosing freelancing as their preferred way of working:

Flexibility and Autonomy

One of the most celebrated aspects of freelancing is the unparalleled flexibility it offers. Freelancers have the autonomy to set their own schedules, choose their work locations, and decide on the volume of work they're comfortable handling. This flexibility allows for a better work-life balance, enabling individuals to tailor their work commitments around personal responsibilities, interests, and peak productivity periods.

Diverse Opportunities

The freelance ecosystem is rich with opportunities across a wide array of industries. From creative endeavors like writing, graphic design, and photography to technical fields such as web development, data analysis, and digital marketing, freelancing opens doors to varied projects and clients. This diversity not only helps in building a multifaceted portfolio but also ensures a stimulating work environment that fosters continuous learning and growth.

Control Over Income and Growth

Freelancing empowers individuals to take control of their income potential. Unlike traditional employment, where salary increments are often predetermined, freelancers can adjust their rates based on experience, skill level, and market demand. Ambitious freelancers can scale their business by taking on more clients or projects, collaborating with others, or offering premium services, thus directly influencing their financial growth.

Pursuit of Passion

Many choose freelancing to pursue work that aligns more closely with their passions and interests. Freelancing provides the freedom to select projects that resonate on a personal level, allowing for a more fulfilling and engaging professional life. This alignment of work with personal interests often results in higher quality outcomes and greater job satisfaction.

Exposure to Global Markets

Freelancing breaks down geographical barriers, offering access to a global client base. This international exposure not only broadens the scope of potential projects but also enriches the freelancer's professional experience through diverse collaborations and insights into global market trends.

Rapid Skill Development

The dynamic nature of freelancing, coupled with the need to stay competitive, propels freelancers into continuous skill development. The diversity of projects and the self-driven quest for market relevance encourage ongoing learning, be it mastering new tools, technologies like AI, or soft skills like client communication and project management.

Entrepreneurial Experience

Freelancing serves as an excellent platform for honing entrepreneurial skills. Managing a freelance business requires wearing multiple hats, from marketing and client relations to finance and project delivery. This hands-on experience is invaluable, laying a solid foundation for those who may aspire to scale their operations into a full-fledged business in the future.

Conclusion

The choice to freelance is driven by a desire for a more personalized, flexible, and fulfilling professional life. While it comes with its set of challenges, the rewards of autonomy, diverse opportunities, and personal growth make freelancing an attractive and viable career path for many. As we delve further into the nuances of freelancing, it becomes evident that success in this domain is not just about talent but also about the strategic utilization of tools and technologies, like AI, to enhance productivity and service offerings.

2.2 The Demand for AI Skills in Freelancing

In the rapidly evolving digital landscape, the demand for AI skills in freelancing has surged, reflecting the broader trend of AI's integration across various industries. This growing demand is fueled by the increasing reliance on data-driven decision-making, automation, and personalized services. Here's a closer look at why AI skills are becoming indispensable for freelancers and how they can tap into this burgeoning market.

The AI Revolution in the Freelance Economy

The freelance economy is not immune to the transformative power of AI. Businesses, from startups to large corporations, are seeking ways to leverage AI to gain a competitive edge, optimize operations, and enhance customer experiences. This shift has created a significant demand for freelancers with AI expertise who can offer specialized skills and solutions.

AI Skills in High Demand

1. **Machine Learning and Data Analysis**: The ability to build and implement machine learning models to analyze large datasets is highly sought after. Freelancers who can extract actionable insights from data are invaluable to clients looking to make informed business decisions.

2. **Natural Language Processing (NLP)**: With the rise of chatbots, virtual assistants, and AI-powered customer service solutions, skills in NLP are increasingly in demand. Freelancers who can develop systems that understand, interpret, and generate human language can tap into a wide range of opportunities.

3. **Computer Vision**: Expertise in computer vision allows freelancers to work on projects involving image and video analysis, facial recognition, and augmented reality applications, among others. This skill is particularly relevant in sectors like security, marketing, and healthcare.

4. **AI-Powered Content Creation**: The ability to use AI tools for generating written content, graphics, and even video content is becoming increasingly popular. Freelancers who can harness these tools can offer efficient and innovative content solutions to their clients.

5. **AI Strategy and Consulting**: Beyond technical implementation, there's a growing need for freelancers who can advise businesses on how to integrate AI into their operations strategically. This includes identifying

opportunities for AI applications, assessing data readiness, and developing AI adoption roadmaps.

Capitalizing on the Demand

1. **Continuous Learning**: The field of AI is continuously evolving, with new tools, frameworks, and best practices emerging regularly. Freelancers need to stay abreast of these developments through online courses, workshops, and industry literature.
2. **Building a Portfolio**: Demonstrating AI skills through a robust portfolio of projects can significantly enhance a freelancer's marketability. This could include case studies, personal projects, or contributions to open-source AI initiatives.
3. **Networking and Community Engagement**: Active participation in AI communities and forums can lead to valuable connections, knowledge exchange, and potential client leads. Freelancers should also consider attending AI conferences and webinars to expand their network.
4. **Specialization**: Given the vastness of the AI field, specializing in a niche area can help freelancers stand out. Whether it's a specific industry application like AI in healthcare or a technology focus like deep learning, specialization can make freelancers more attractive to clients looking for expert skills.

Conclusion

The demand for AI skills in freelancing reflects the broader trend of digital transformation across industries. For freelancers, this presents a golden opportunity to leverage their AI expertise or upskill in AI technologies to meet market demands. By staying informed, continuously learning, and strategically marketing their skills, freelancers can capitalize on the AI revolution to enhance their offerings and secure a competitive edge in the dynamic freelance marketplace.

2.3 Setting Up Your Freelance Business Foundation

Transitioning into freelancing or scaling your freelance operations requires more than just expertise in your field; it necessitates a solid business foundation. This foundation is crucial for sustaining and growing your freelance career in the long term. Here's how to establish a strong base for your freelance business:

Define Your Niche and Services

Start by clearly defining your niche and the services you offer. This specificity helps in targeting the right clients and differentiating yourself in a crowded market. For freelancers with AI skills, this could mean focusing on particular AI applications like machine learning development, AI-driven content creation, or AI strategy consulting.

Legal and Administrative Setup

Ensure your freelance business is legally compliant by registering your business, if necessary, in your jurisdiction. This might involve choosing a business structure (such as sole proprietorship, LLC, etc.), obtaining necessary licenses or permits, and understanding your tax obligations. Additionally, setting up a separate business bank account can help keep personal and business finances distinct, simplifying accounting and tax processes.

Branding and Online Presence

Your brand is your freelance business's identity and promise to your clients. Invest time in creating a professional brand that reflects your expertise and values. This includes a memorable business name, a professional logo, and a portfolio website showcasing your work and testimonials. Your online presence, especially on professional networks like LinkedIn and industry-specific platforms, is vital for networking and attracting clients.

Set Clear Rates and Payment Terms

Determine your pricing structure based on your expertise, market rates, and the value you deliver. Whether you charge by the hour, project, or value-based pricing, be transparent with your rates and communicate them clearly to potential clients. Establishing clear payment terms, including invoicing procedures, payment timelines, and late payment policies, is also crucial to ensure smooth financial operations.

Tools and Systems for Efficiency

Leverage technology to streamline your operations and enhance productivity. This includes project management tools, time tracking software, accounting software, and communication platforms. For AI-focused freelancers, staying updated with the latest AI tools and platforms that can aid in your projects is essential.

Continuous Learning and Development

The freelance landscape, especially in fields like AI, is constantly evolving. Commit to ongoing learning to keep your skills sharp and your services competitive. This can involve formal education, online courses, webinars, and staying active in professional communities.

Marketing and Client Acquisition

Develop a marketing strategy that highlights your unique selling points and reaches your target audience. This could include content marketing, social media engagement, networking events, and leveraging freelance marketplaces. Building relationships with clients and encouraging referrals and repeat business are also key components of a successful freelance marketing strategy.

Financial Planning and Stability

Financial stability is crucial for the ebbs and flows of freelance work. This involves setting aside savings for lean periods, investing in insurance (health, professional liability, etc.), and planning for taxes. Creating a budget and regularly reviewing your financial health can help you make informed decisions about your business.

Conclusion

Setting up a solid foundation for your freelance business involves careful planning and attention to detail across various aspects, from legal and administrative to marketing and financial planning. For freelancers in the AI domain, it's equally important to stay at the forefront of technological advancements and continuously refine your offerings. With a strong foundation, you can navigate the freelance world with confidence, delivering exceptional value to your clients while growing your business.

Chapter 3: Essential AI Tools for Freelancers

In the rapidly evolving field of freelancing, staying ahead of the technological curve is crucial. Artificial Intelligence (AI) offers a suite of tools that can enhance productivity, creativity, and service delivery for freelancers across various sectors. This chapter explores essential AI tools that can be instrumental in elevating your freelance business.

AI Tools for Productivity

1. **Project Management**: AI-powered project management tools like *Asana* and *Trello* use AI to automate task assignments, set deadlines, and predict project timelines, helping freelancers stay organized and meet deadlines.
2. **Time Management and Tracking**: Tools like *RescueTime* and *Toggl* employ AI to track time spent on tasks, offering insights into productivity patterns and suggesting improvements.
3. **Email Management**: AI-driven email clients like *Superhuman* and *Astro* help manage inboxes efficiently, prioritizing important emails and automating responses, saving valuable time.

AI Tools for Creativity

1. **Content Creation**: Platforms like *OpenAI's GPT-3* for writing assistance and *Canva's* design suggestions use

AI to enhance content creation, from drafting articles to designing graphics.

2. **Image and Video Editing**: Tools such as *Adobe Photoshop's* AI features and *Lumen5* for video creation leverage AI to simplify complex editing tasks, allowing freelancers to produce high-quality visuals with minimal effort.
3. **Music and Audio Production**: AI platforms like *Amper Music* and *AIVA* enable freelancers to compose custom music and enhance audio quality, perfect for multimedia projects.

AI Tools for Data Analysis and Decision Making

1. **Data Analysis**: Tools like *Tableau* and *Microsoft Power BI* integrate AI to help freelancers analyze and visualize data for their clients, uncovering insights that drive decision-making.
2. **Market Research**: AI-driven tools like *Crayon* and *Brand24* offer market intelligence and sentiment analysis, assisting freelancers in understanding market trends and consumer preferences.

AI Tools for Communication and Customer Service

1. **Chatbots and Virtual Assistants**: Platforms like *Intercom* and *Drift* use AI to power chatbots and virtual assistants, helping freelancers provide instant customer support and lead generation services.
2. **Language Translation**: Tools like *DeepL* and *Google Translate* leverage AI for accurate and context-aware

language translation, invaluable for freelancers working with international clients.

AI Tools for Security

1. **Cybersecurity**: AI-powered security tools like *CrowdStrike* and *Darktrace* offer advanced threat detection and response capabilities, ensuring freelancers' and their clients' data remains secure.

Leveraging AI Tools Effectively

To make the most of these AI tools, freelancers should:

- **Identify specific needs**: Choose AI tools that address your unique challenges and fit seamlessly into your workflow.
- **Stay updated**: AI technology evolves rapidly, so keeping abreast of the latest tools and features can give you a competitive edge.
- **Balance AI with human touch**: While AI can enhance efficiency and quality, the human element—creativity, empathy, and personal judgment—remains irreplaceable in freelancing.

Conclusion

AI tools offer a realm of possibilities for freelancers to enhance their work, improve productivity, and deliver exceptional value to clients. By strategically integrating these tools into their business, freelancers can not only streamline their operations but also open up new avenues for innovation and creativity in their services.

3.1 AI Tools for Efficiency and Productivity

For freelancers, maximizing efficiency and productivity isn't just about working harder; it's about working smarter. Artificial Intelligence (AI) tools are game-changers in this arena, automating routine tasks, optimizing workflows, and providing insights that help freelancers manage their time and resources more effectively. Here's a closer look at some AI tools that can significantly boost efficiency and productivity for freelancers.

Task Automation and Workflow Optimization

- **Zapier**: This tool automates workflows by connecting your favorite apps and services, allowing you to automate repetitive tasks without coding. For instance, Zapier can automatically save email attachments to a cloud storage service or sync new tasks across different project management tools.
- **IFTTT (If This Then That)**: Similar to Zapier, IFTTT automates actions between web services and devices. For example, it can automatically tweet your blog posts or adjust your calendar based on your to-do list.

Project Management and Collaboration

- **Trello with Butler**: Trello's built-in automation tool, Butler, uses natural language commands to automate actions within your boards, lists, and cards. This can range from assigning tasks to team members based on the card's status to scheduling due date reminders.

- **Asana**: Leveraging AI, Asana helps manage projects and tasks in one tool, offering features like workload management to balance tasks among team members and predicting project completion dates.

Time Management and Tracking

- **Timely**: This AI-powered time tracking tool automatically records the time you spend on different tasks and projects. It uses AI to categorize your work and provide insights into how you can work more efficiently.
- **RescueTime**: By running securely in the background on your computer and mobile devices, RescueTime tracks time spent on applications and websites, giving you an accurate picture of your day. It offers detailed reports and data to help you understand your time management and productivity patterns.

Email Management and Scheduling

- **Boomerang for Gmail**: Boomerang uses AI to help you schedule emails, set up follow-up reminders, and even suggest email responses. Its AI-driven feature, Respondable, provides real-time feedback on your email's effectiveness.
- **x.ai**: This AI scheduling tool coordinates meetings for you by connecting with your calendar. You simply cc "Amy" or "Andrew" in your emails, and the AI handles

all the back-and-forth communication to find a suitable meeting time for all parties.

Note-Taking and Organization

- **Evernote**: With its AI-powered features, Evernote becomes more than just a note-taking app. It can automatically categorize your notes, suggest related content, and even turn handwritten notes into searchable text.
- **Otter.ai**: This tool transcribes meetings, lectures, interviews, or any voice conversations in real-time, allowing freelancers to focus on the discussion without worrying about taking notes. It also generates searchable, shareable transcripts.

Conclusion

Incorporating AI tools into your freelancing toolkit can significantly enhance your efficiency and productivity. By automating routine tasks, managing your projects more effectively, and gaining insights into your work patterns, you can free up valuable time to focus on high-value activities and grow your freelance business. As AI technology continues to evolve, staying abreast of new tools and features will ensure you remain competitive in the fast-paced freelance market.

3.2 Managing Projects and Deadlines with AI

For freelancers, juggling multiple projects and deadlines is a daily reality. Efficient project management not only ensures the timely delivery of high-quality work but also helps maintain a healthy work-life balance. Artificial Intelligence (AI) can play a pivotal role in streamlining project management and deadline tracking, offering smart solutions that adapt to your workflow. Here's how AI can assist freelancers in managing their projects and deadlines more effectively.

AI-Driven Project Management Tools

- **Monday.com**: This tool leverages AI to provide insights into project timelines, workload distribution, and potential bottlenecks. Its AI features can predict project risks and suggest adjustments to keep everything on track.
- **Wrike**: Wrike uses AI to automate task prioritization, suggest project timelines based on historical data, and even recommend task assignments based on team members' past performance and current workload.
- **ClickUp**: With features like task automation and AI-driven time estimates, ClickUp helps freelancers manage tasks more efficiently. Its AI capabilities can also predict task durations based on your history, helping you set more accurate deadlines.

Deadline Tracking and Prioritization

- **Toggl Plan**: This tool uses AI to help freelancers visualize their project timelines and deadlines on a shared calendar. Its AI component can suggest task timelines and help adjust schedules dynamically as priorities change.
- **Todoist**: Todoist's AI learns your task management habits and can automatically suggest due dates and

priority levels for new tasks, making it easier to stay on top of deadlines.

AI for Efficient Time Allocation

- **Forecast.app**: This AI-powered tool helps freelancers allocate their time more efficiently across projects. It analyzes your project history and current workload to provide realistic time estimates for tasks, ensuring you don't overcommit.
- **Timely**: By automatically tracking the time you spend on different tasks and projects, Timely's AI provides insights into how you work and offers suggestions for optimizing your schedule.

Automating Repetitive Tasks

- **Zapier**: Zapier's automation capabilities can be used to streamline repetitive project management tasks, such as updating project boards, scheduling meetings, or sending project updates to clients.
- **IFTTT**: Similar to Zapier, IFTTT can automate various tasks related to project management, from setting reminders based on project deadlines to syncing tasks across different platforms.

Enhancing Communication and Collaboration

- **Slack**: With its AI-driven features, Slack can prioritize messages, suggest responses, and even summarize conversations, making team communication more efficient.

- **Microsoft Teams**: Teams uses AI to transcribe meetings, translate languages in real-time, and offer post-meeting summaries, ensuring clear communication and collaboration across global freelance teams.

Conclusion

Leveraging AI in project management and deadline tracking allows freelancers to work smarter, not harder. By automating routine tasks, efficiently allocating time, and providing actionable insights, AI tools help freelancers stay organized, meet deadlines, and deliver quality work. As AI technology continues to advance, embracing these tools can significantly enhance a freelancer's productivity and overall business success.

3.3 Enhancing Communication with AI

Effective communication is the cornerstone of successful freelancing, involving clear interactions with clients, collaborators, and even potential leads. In the digital age, AI is revolutionizing the way freelancers communicate, making processes more efficient and interactions more impactful. Here's how AI can enhance communication for freelancers:

AI-Powered Email and Messaging Tools

- **Grammarly**: Beyond basic grammar checks, Grammarly uses AI to analyze the tone and clarity of your emails and messages, ensuring your communication is professional and aligns with the intended message. It

also suggests style improvements to make your writing more engaging.
- **Boomerang for Gmail**: Boomerang's AI-powered features, like Respondable, analyze your emails for readability, politeness, and response likelihood, helping you craft emails that are more likely to receive positive responses.

Virtual Assistants for Scheduling

- **x.ai**: This AI virtual assistant automates meeting scheduling by handling email negotiations to find suitable times for all parties, freeing up your time for more productive work.
- **Google Assistant**: For freelancers using Google Workspace, Google Assistant can help manage your calendar, set reminders, and even send emails or messages through voice commands, streamlining your communication tasks.

AI-Driven Customer Service Solutions

- **Zendesk Answer Bot**: This tool uses AI to provide instant, automated responses to common customer inquiries, ensuring clients receive timely support. It can be integrated into email, chat, or even social media platforms.
- **Intercom**: Intercom's AI-powered chatbots can engage website visitors, answer FAQs, and even qualify leads, ensuring potential clients get the information they need quickly.

Real-Time Language Translation

- **DeepL**: DeepL offers highly accurate, context-aware translations, enabling freelancers to communicate seamlessly with international clients, breaking down language barriers.
- **Google Translate**: With its document translation features and real-time conversation mode, Google Translate facilitates communication in multiple languages, broadening the scope for international projects.

Enhancing Voice Communications

- **Otter.ai**: Otter.ai transcribes live conversations and meetings in real-time, providing written records that can be shared with clients or team members, ensuring clarity and accountability in verbal communications.
- **Descript**: Descript offers AI-powered transcription, editing, and overdubbing for audio and video content, making it easier for freelancers to produce and share multimedia communications with clients.

Conclusion

AI is transforming the landscape of freelance communication, offering tools that not only streamline administrative tasks like scheduling and email management but also enhance the quality of interactions. By leveraging AI-driven writing assistants, virtual assistants, customer service bots, and real-time translation services, freelancers can communicate more effectively, ensuring messages are clear, professional, and timely. As the digital workplace continues to evolve, integrating AI into communication strategies will be key for freelancers looking to maintain and grow their client relationships and collaborations.

Chapter 4: AI Skills That Pay the Bills

In the rapidly evolving freelance marketplace, Artificial Intelligence (AI) skills are not just in demand; they are becoming essential for those looking to stay competitive and capture high-value projects. This chapter delves into the AI skills that are particularly lucrative in the freelance world, offering insights on how to develop these skills and apply them to create impactful, income-generating work.

Machine Learning Development

Machine learning, a subset of AI, involves creating algorithms that enable computers to learn from and make predictions or decisions based on data. Freelancers with skills in developing, training, and deploying machine learning models are in high demand across industries, from finance and healthcare to marketing and e-commerce.

- **Key Skills**: Proficiency in programming languages like Python or R, understanding of ML algorithms and neural networks, and experience with ML frameworks such as TensorFlow or PyTorch.
- **Applications**: Predictive analytics, customer behavior analysis, personalization engines, and more.

Natural Language Processing (NLP)

NLP involves programming computers to process and analyze large amounts of natural language data, enabling them to understand and generate human language. Skills in NLP are sought after for projects involving chatbots, voice assistants, sentiment analysis, and content generation.

- **Key Skills**: Understanding of linguistics and language models, experience with NLP libraries like NLTK or SpaCy, and familiarity with text analysis and generation techniques.
- **Applications**: Chatbots, customer service automation, content summarization, language translation services.

Computer Vision

Computer vision enables machines to interpret and make decisions based on visual data. Freelancers skilled in computer vision can work on projects ranging from facial recognition systems to augmented reality applications.

- **Key Skills**: Expertise in image processing techniques, knowledge of computer vision libraries like OpenCV, and experience with deep learning approaches for image classification and object detection.
- **Applications**: Security and surveillance, quality control in manufacturing, retail analytics, and interactive marketing experiences.

AI-Powered Analytics

The ability to harness AI for deep data analysis allows freelancers to provide actionable insights that can drive business strategies. This skill set is particularly valuable in fields like marketing, finance, and healthcare.

- **Key Skills**: Proficiency in data analysis tools and platforms, understanding of predictive modeling and statistical analysis, and the ability to translate data insights into strategic recommendations.
- **Applications**: Market trend analysis, financial forecasting, healthcare data analysis, and targeted marketing strategies.

Developing and Deploying AI Models

Freelancers who can not only develop AI models but also deploy them into production environments are highly sought after. This involves knowledge of cloud platforms, containerization, and model monitoring and maintenance.

- **Key Skills**: Experience with cloud services like AWS, Azure, or Google Cloud, understanding of container technologies like Docker, and familiarity with CI/CD pipelines.
- **Applications**: Deploying AI applications, maintaining AI services in production, and ensuring model reliability and scalability.

How to Develop AI Skills

- **Online Courses and Certifications**: Platforms like Coursera, Udacity, and edX offer specialized courses in AI, machine learning, and data science, taught by industry experts.
- **Hands-On Projects**: Applying what you learn through personal projects or contributions to open-source AI projects can solidify your skills and build your portfolio.
- **Continuous Learning**: The field of AI is constantly evolving, so staying updated with the latest research, tools, and best practices is crucial.

Conclusion

For freelancers, developing AI skills is not just about staying relevant; it's about positioning oneself at the forefront of technological innovation and tapping into high-value project opportunities. By focusing on in-demand AI skills and continually honing and applying these skills, freelancers can create a niche for themselves that pays the bills and sets the stage for a thriving, future-proof career.

4.1 In-Demand AI Skills for Freelancers

In the dynamic world of freelancing, Artificial Intelligence (AI) has emerged as a field rich with opportunity. As businesses across sectors seek to leverage AI for competitive advantage, the demand for freelancers with specialized AI skills has surged. Here are some of the most in-demand AI skills that freelancers can develop to capitalize on this growing market.

Machine Learning (ML) Development

Understanding and implementing ML models is a highly sought-after skill. Freelancers who can build predictive models, perform data mining, and apply deep learning techniques are in demand for projects ranging from customer behavior analysis to autonomous systems.

- **Skills to Master**: Python or R programming, TensorFlow or PyTorch, data preprocessing, and neural networks.

Natural Language Processing (NLP)

With the proliferation of chatbots, voice assistants, and AI-driven content creation, NLP skills are increasingly valuable. Freelancers skilled in NLP can work on projects involving sentiment analysis, language translation, and automated content generation.

- **Skills to Master**: Text analysis, sentiment analysis, language modeling, and familiarity with NLP libraries like NLTK or SpaCy.

Computer Vision

Computer vision skills allow freelancers to engage in projects that require the interpretation of visual data, such as image recognition, object detection, and augmented reality applications.

- **Skills to Master**: Image processing techniques, OpenCV, convolutional neural networks (CNNs), and real-time video analysis.

Data Analysis and Visualization

The ability to analyze and visualize data using AI and machine learning algorithms is crucial for extracting actionable insights. Freelancers with these skills can help businesses make data-driven decisions.

- **Skills to Master**: Statistical analysis, data modeling, Python libraries like Pandas and Matplotlib, and data visualization tools like Tableau or Power BI.

AI Model Deployment and Cloud Computing

Deploying AI models into production environments is a critical step in the AI development process. Freelancers who understand cloud computing and model deployment can offer end-to-end AI solutions.

- **Skills to Master**: Cloud platforms (AWS, Azure, Google Cloud), containerization (Docker, Kubernetes), and CI/CD pipelines.

AI Ethics and Bias Mitigation

As AI becomes more integrated into products and services, understanding the ethical implications and how to mitigate biases in AI models is becoming increasingly important.

- **Skills to Master**: Ethical AI principles, bias detection techniques, and fairness in machine learning models.

Robotic Process Automation (RPA)

RPA involves automating routine business processes with software robots. Freelancers with RPA skills can help businesses automate tasks, improving efficiency and accuracy.

- **Skills to Master**: RPA tools like UiPath or Automation Anywhere, workflow design, and process optimization.

How to Develop These Skills

1. **Online Learning**: Platforms like Coursera, Udacity, and edX offer courses and specializations in AI, ML, NLP, and more, often designed by industry experts and leading universities.
2. **Practical Experience**: Engage in hands-on projects, contribute to open-source AI projects, or participate in hackathons and competitions to apply your skills in real-world scenarios.
3. **Professional Networking**: Join AI-focused online communities, attend webinars and conferences, and connect with other AI professionals to stay updated on industry trends and opportunities.

Conclusion

For freelancers looking to thrive in the AI space, developing and continuously updating these in-demand skills is key. By aligning your expertise with market needs, you can position yourself as a valuable asset to clients, commanding higher rates and engaging in cutting-edge projects that shape the future of technology.

4.2 Learning and Improving Your AI Skills

As the demand for AI expertise continues to grow, freelancers must focus on acquiring and refining their AI skills to remain competitive in the market. Continuous learning and skill improvement are essential for staying abreast of the latest technologies and methodologies in AI. Here are effective strategies for learning and enhancing your AI capabilities.

Engage with Online Learning Platforms

Online courses and tutorials offer a flexible and accessible way to learn AI from scratch or deepen your existing knowledge. Platforms like Coursera, Udacity, edX, and Khan Academy host courses designed by experts from leading universities and tech companies, covering a broad spectrum of AI topics from beginner to advanced levels.

- **Action Steps**: Enroll in courses that match your skill level and interests. Set a regular learning schedule, and apply the concepts through practical projects.

Participate in AI Bootcamps and Workshops

Bootcamps and workshops provide intensive, hands-on learning experiences, often led by industry professionals. These programs are designed to equip you with practical skills and real-world project experience in a short period.

- **Action Steps**: Research reputable AI bootcamps that offer programs in your area of interest. Look for ones that provide mentorship, career services, and opportunities to work on live projects.

Join AI Communities and Forums

Communities and forums bring together AI enthusiasts and professionals to discuss trends, challenges, and opportunities. Platforms like GitHub, Stack Overflow, Reddit (subreddits like r/MachineLearning), and specialized AI forums offer valuable resources and networking opportunities.

- **Action Steps**: Actively participate in discussions, ask questions, and share your insights. Collaborate on open-source projects to gain practical experience and contribute to the AI community.

Attend Conferences and Webinars

AI conferences, seminars, and webinars are excellent sources of cutting-edge knowledge, showcasing the latest research, tools, and case studies from the field. They also offer networking opportunities with fellow AI professionals and industry leaders.

- **Action Steps**: Keep an eye out for AI conferences and webinars relevant to your interests. Many events offer virtual attendance options, making them more accessible.

Practice Through Real-World Projects

Applying AI concepts to real-world problems is one of the most effective ways to solidify your understanding and develop practical skills. Freelance projects, personal projects, or contributions to open-source AI initiatives can all provide valuable hands-on experience.

- **Action Steps**: Identify problems you're passionate about solving with AI. Use platforms like Kaggle to find datasets and challenges that align with your interests.

Stay Updated with AI Research and Publications

AI is a rapidly evolving field, with new research and developments emerging regularly. Staying informed about the latest findings, techniques, and best practices is crucial for keeping your skills current.

- **Action Steps**: Follow AI research journals, blogs, and influencers. Platforms like arXiv and Google Scholar are excellent resources for accessing AI research papers.

Seek Mentorship and Peer Feedback

Learning from experienced AI professionals can accelerate your growth and help you navigate challenges more effectively. Similarly, peer feedback on your projects can provide new perspectives and insights.

- **Action Steps**: Reach out to potential mentors within your network or through professional platforms like

LinkedIn. Participate in peer review sessions in online forums or local meetups.

Conclusion

Developing and improving AI skills is a journey of continuous learning and practice. By leveraging online resources, engaging with the AI community, and applying your knowledge to real-world problems, you can build a robust skillset that sets you apart in the freelance marketplace. Remember, the key to success in AI is not just in mastering the technical aspects but also in staying adaptable and curious in the face of rapid technological advancements.

4.3 Showcasing Your Skills: Building a Portfolio

For freelancers in the AI domain, a well-crafted portfolio is crucial for attracting clients and demonstrating the breadth and depth of your skills. A portfolio not only showcases your past work but also provides tangible proof of your expertise and problem-solving abilities. Here's how you can build an impactful AI portfolio that stands out.

Start with a Strong Foundation

- **Personal Website**: Create a professional website that serves as the central hub for your portfolio. Include an about section, your resume, contact information, and, most importantly, your portfolio projects.
- **Clear, Concise Descriptions**: For each project in your portfolio, include a clear and concise description that covers the problem statement, your solution approach,

the AI technologies and techniques used, and the project outcome.

Highlight a Range of Projects

- **Diversity**: Showcase a variety of projects that demonstrate a broad range of AI skills, from machine learning models and NLP applications to computer vision projects. This diversity will appeal to a wider range of potential clients.
- **Depth**: Include one or two deep-dive projects that showcase your ability to tackle complex problems and deliver sophisticated AI solutions. These flagship projects can significantly boost your credibility.

Include Real-World Applications

- **Client Projects**: If you've completed AI projects for clients and have permission to share, include these in your portfolio to demonstrate your real-world experience and success in delivering client solutions.
- **Personal Projects**: Don't hesitate to include personal or passion projects that highlight your initiative, creativity, and ability to apply AI to solve unique problems.

Demonstrate Your Process

- **Problem-Solving Approach**: Clearly articulate your problem-solving approach, from understanding the problem and data preprocessing to model selection, training, and evaluation. This demonstrates your methodical and analytical approach to potential clients.

- **Visuals and Demos**: Where possible, include visuals such as charts, graphs, or even short video demos to make your projects more engaging and easier to understand.

Leverage Open Source and Collaborative Projects

- **GitHub**: Maintain an active GitHub profile where you can host your project code, especially for personal or open-source projects. This allows potential clients to delve into your coding practices and contributions.
- **Contributions to Open Source**: Highlight your contributions to open-source AI projects or libraries. This not only shows your technical skills but also your ability to collaborate within the AI community.

Keep It Updated

- **Regular Updates**: Keep your portfolio fresh by regularly adding new projects and updating existing ones with new insights or improvements.
- **Continuous Learning**: Reflect your commitment to continuous learning by including projects that utilize the latest AI technologies and techniques.

Promote Your Portfolio

- **Professional Networks**: Share your portfolio on professional networking sites like LinkedIn, and engage

with AI and freelancing communities to increase
visibility.

- **Content Creation**: Consider blogging about your
projects or sharing project case studies, which can drive
traffic to your portfolio and establish your thought
leadership in the AI domain.

Conclusion

A well-constructed AI portfolio is a dynamic tool that not only
showcases your technical expertise but also your problem-
solving capabilities, creativity, and ability to deliver tangible
results. By carefully selecting and presenting your projects,
you can create a compelling narrative that highlights your
value as a freelancer in the AI space, attracting clients and
opportunities that align with your skills and interests.

Chapter 5: Finding AI Freelance Work

Securing freelance work in the AI domain requires a proactive approach and strategic positioning in the market. As AI continues to transform industries, opportunities for freelancers with AI expertise are expanding. This chapter provides guidance on navigating the freelance landscape to find rewarding AI projects.

Leverage Freelance Platforms

Freelance platforms like Upwork, Freelancer, and Toptal are popular places where clients post AI-related projects. These platforms offer a wide range of opportunities, from short-term tasks to long-term collaborations.

- **Optimize Your Profile**: Highlight your AI skills, certifications, and portfolio. Use keywords related to AI technologies and applications to increase your visibility in search results.
- **Bid Strategically**: Tailor your proposals to each project, highlighting how your AI expertise can solve the client's problem. Be competitive with your rates without undervaluing your skills.

Utilize Professional Networking Sites

LinkedIn is a powerful tool for professional networking and job searching. It allows you to connect with industry professionals, join AI-focused groups, and apply for freelance roles advertised on the platform.

- **Active Engagement**: Share your insights, projects, and achievements related to AI. Engaging with content from other AI professionals can increase your visibility and attract potential clients.
- **Direct Outreach**: Don't hesitate to reach out to companies or individuals who might benefit from your AI expertise. A well-crafted, personalized message can open doors to freelance opportunities.

Participate in AI Communities and Forums

Joining AI communities and forums such as GitHub, Stack Overflow, Reddit (e.g., r/MachineLearning), and specialized AI forums can help you stay updated on industry trends, network with peers, and find freelance opportunities.

- **Contribute and Collaborate**: Actively participating in discussions, contributing to open-source projects, and collaborating on challenges can showcase your skills and lead to freelance project offers.

Attend AI Conferences and Workshops

AI conferences, workshops, and meetups provide excellent networking opportunities. They allow you to meet potential clients, learn about the latest AI advancements, and showcase your expertise.

- **Networking**: Prepare an elevator pitch about your freelance services. Collect business cards and follow up with contacts post-event.
- **Presentations and Hackathons**: Participating in or speaking at these events can significantly raise your profile and attract freelance offers.

Build an Online Presence

A strong online presence can attract clients to you. Maintain an active blog, contribute to AI publications, or create video content that demonstrates your AI knowledge and projects.

- **Content Marketing**: Share insights on AI trends, case studies, or tutorials. High-quality content can establish you as an authority in the AI field and attract clients looking for experts.

Offer Consultation Services

Many businesses are looking to integrate AI into their operations but lack the expertise to do so effectively. Offering AI consultation services can be a lucrative avenue for freelancers with a deep understanding of AI applications and industry knowledge.

- **Identify Target Markets**: Focus on industries where AI adoption is growing, such as healthcare, finance, or e-commerce.
- **Promotional Offers**: Consider offering a free initial consultation to showcase the value you can bring to a business.

Conclusion

Finding freelance work in AI involves a combination of showcasing your expertise, strategic networking, and active participation in the AI community. By leveraging multiple channels and continuously enhancing your skills and portfolio, you can secure rewarding freelance opportunities and build a successful career in the burgeoning field of AI.

5.1 Platforms for AI Freelancers

Navigating the freelance landscape for AI professionals involves knowing where to look for opportunities. Several platforms cater specifically to tech and AI freelancers, offering a range of projects from startups to large corporations. Here's a guide to some of the key platforms where AI freelancers can find work and how to effectively use them.

Upwork

Upwork is one of the largest global freelancing platforms, with a wide array of AI-related projects. From machine learning models to data analysis and NLP projects, Upwork offers diverse opportunities for AI professionals.

- **Optimizing Your Profile**: Highlight your AI skills and certifications, and make sure to include a portfolio of relevant projects. Use keywords related to your AI expertise in your profile to improve visibility.
- **Proposal Writing**: Tailor your proposals to each job post, clearly articulating how your skills can address the client's specific needs.

Toptal

Toptal prides itself on connecting top freelance talent with companies, and it has a rigorous screening process. It's an excellent platform for experienced AI freelancers looking for high-quality projects.

- **Getting Accepted**: Prepare for a thorough vetting process, including language and personality tests, in-depth skill reviews, and live screening tasks.
- **Building Reputation**: Once in, maintain high standards to get noticed by premium clients. Engage in Toptal community events and webinars to enhance your visibility.

Kaggle

Kaggle is known for its data science competitions, but it's also a platform where businesses post data-related jobs, including AI projects. Participating in competitions can showcase your skills and attract freelance offers.

- **Competition Participation**: Use competitions as a way to demonstrate your expertise in solving real-world problems with AI. Highlight your Kaggle achievements on your personal website or LinkedIn profile.
- **Kaggle Jobs Board**: Check the Kaggle jobs board for AI freelance opportunities posted by companies engaged with the Kaggle community.

GitHub

While primarily a platform for hosting code, GitHub can serve as a portfolio for your AI projects. Actively contributing to open-source AI projects can also lead to freelance opportunities.

- **Showcase Your Work**: Ensure your GitHub profile is up-to-date with your AI projects, clearly documented, and includes a README file explaining each project's purpose and functionality.
- **Community Engagement**: Contribute to popular AI repositories, engage with other developers, and participate in discussions to increase your visibility within the GitHub community.

AngelList

AngelList caters to startups, many of which are keen on incorporating AI into their products and services. It's an ideal platform for freelancers looking to work with innovative companies on cutting-edge AI projects.

- **Startup Collaboration**: Emphasize your ability to work in fast-paced environments and your passion for innovation in your profile.
- **Direct Approach**: Proactively reach out to startups that interest you, even if they haven't posted a job listing, offering your AI expertise.

LinkedIn

LinkedIn's job board often lists freelance AI opportunities, and its networking capabilities allow you to connect directly with potential clients in your industry.

- **Profile Optimization**: Use AI-related keywords throughout your profile, and regularly update your accomplishments and project portfolio.
- **Active Engagement**: Publish articles, share insights on AI trends, and engage with content from industry leaders to increase your visibility.

Conclusion

Leveraging these platforms requires more than just signing up; it involves actively showcasing your skills, engaging with the community, and tailoring your outreach to potential clients. By strategically positioning yourself on these platforms, you can access a wide range of AI freelance opportunities suited to your expertise and career goals.

5.2 Pitching and Securing AI Projects

Successfully pitching and securing AI projects as a freelancer involves more than just technical expertise; it requires a strategic approach to communication and negotiation. Understanding the client's needs, presenting your skills effectively, and building trust are key components of a successful pitch. Here are strategies to enhance your pitching process and increase your chances of securing AI projects.

Understand the Client's Needs

Before crafting your pitch, take the time to thoroughly understand the client's problem or project requirements. Review the project description carefully, research the client's industry, and prepare any questions that can clarify the project scope and goals.

- **Action Steps**: Use the initial communication or proposal submission to ask insightful questions that demonstrate your interest and understanding of the project.

Tailor Your Pitch

Generic pitches rarely stand out. Customize your proposal to address the specific needs and pain points of the client, highlighting how your AI expertise can provide the ideal solution.

- **Action Steps**: Refer to similar past projects in your pitch, and briefly outline your proposed approach to solving the client's problem. Include any relevant case studies or portfolio items that showcase your ability to deliver similar solutions.

Highlight Your Unique Value Proposition

What makes you the best choice for this project? Your unique value proposition (UVP) could be your specialized expertise in a particular AI domain, your proven track record of successful projects, or your innovative approach to problem-solving.

- **Action Steps**: Clearly articulate your UVP in your pitch, focusing on how it benefits the client and sets you apart from other freelancers.

Communicate Clearly and Concisely

Clients often review multiple proposals, so clarity and conciseness are crucial. Clearly outline your understanding of the project, your proposed solution, and the expected outcomes, avoiding jargon and overly technical language unless necessary.

- **Action Steps**: Use bullet points or numbered lists to make your proposal easy to scan. Highlight key points such as project milestones, timelines, and deliverables.

Showcase Your Technical Competency

While you should avoid unnecessary jargon, it's important to reassure clients of your technical competency. Briefly mention the technologies, methodologies, or frameworks you plan to use and why they're suited for the project.

- **Action Steps**: If applicable, include links to your GitHub repository, technical blog, or portfolio website where clients can see examples of your work.

Build Trust through Transparency

Building trust is essential, especially for complex and potentially high-stakes AI projects. Be transparent about your capabilities, availability, and any potential challenges you foresee. Setting realistic expectations helps build client trust and reduces the risk of issues down the line.

- **Action Steps**: Be honest about what you can deliver and by when. If there are any uncertainties or risks associated with the project, discuss them openly and propose potential mitigation strategies.

Follow Up

Persistence can pay off. If you haven't heard back from a client after submitting your proposal, a polite follow-up can demonstrate your continued interest in the project and keep you top of mind.

- **Action Steps**: Send a follow-up message or email a week after your initial proposal, reiterating your interest in the project and asking if there are any additional questions you can answer.

Conclusion

Securing AI freelance projects requires a combination of understanding the client's needs, effectively communicating your expertise and proposed solutions, and building trust. Tailoring your pitch, showcasing your technical skills, and maintaining open and honest communication are key to converting proposals into successful project engagements.

5.3 Networking and Building Client Relationships

For AI freelancers, networking isn't just about expanding your list of contacts; it's about building meaningful relationships that can lead to long-term collaborations and referrals. Similarly, maintaining strong relationships with existing clients is crucial for repeat business and a steady stream of projects. Here's how you can effectively network and nurture client relationships in the AI freelance market.

Effective Networking Strategies

- **Attend Industry Events**: Conferences, seminars, and meetups related to AI and tech are great opportunities to meet potential clients and collaborators. Engage actively by asking questions, participating in discussions, and sharing your insights.
- **Online Communities and Forums**: Participate in AI-related forums, LinkedIn groups, and other online communities. Share your expertise, answer questions, and engage in conversations to raise your profile.
- **Collaborate on Projects**: Working on open-source projects or collaborating with other professionals on projects can expand your network and expose you to potential clients.
- **Alumni and Professional Associations**: Leverage alumni networks from your educational institutions and memberships in professional associations to connect with peers and industry professionals.

Building and Maintaining Client Relationships

- **Understand Their Business**: Take the time to understand your clients' business goals, challenges, and industry trends. This shows that you're invested in their success beyond just completing a project.
- **Clear Communication**: Keep clients updated on project progress, potential challenges, and successes. Regular, transparent communication builds trust and confidence in your working relationship.
- **Deliver Consistently High-Quality Work**: The quality of your work is a direct reflection of your professionalism. Consistently delivering high-quality, timely work is the best way to maintain a positive relationship with clients.
- **Ask for Feedback**: After project completion, ask clients for feedback. This not only provides valuable insights for improvement but also shows that you value their opinion and are committed to excellence.
- **Provide Value Beyond the Contract**: Share relevant articles, reports, and insights with your clients that might benefit their business. This helps position you as a trusted advisor, not just a service provider.
- **Follow Up and Stay in Touch**: Even after a project is completed, check in with past clients periodically. Share updates on your work or insights relevant to their business. Keeping the communication lines open can lead to repeat business or referrals.

Leveraging Social Media for Networking

- **LinkedIn**: Regularly update your profile with recent projects, articles, and achievements. Publish posts and articles related to AI to showcase your expertise. Engage with your connections' content to stay visible in their networks.
- **Twitter**: Follow industry leaders, join conversations on AI topics, and share your own projects and insights. Twitter chats can be a dynamic way to engage with the AI community.
- **Personal Blog or Website**: Regularly publishing blog posts on your website about AI trends, project case studies, or tutorials can attract potential clients and demonstrate your expertise and thought leadership in the field.

Conclusion

Effective networking and client relationship management are pivotal for AI freelancers seeking to build a sustainable and thriving freelance career. By actively engaging in the professional community, delivering exceptional work, and maintaining open lines of communication with clients, you can establish a strong network that supports your freelance journey in the long term.

Chapter 6: Pricing Your AI Freelance Services

Setting the right price for your AI freelance services is crucial for ensuring that you are fairly compensated for your expertise while remaining competitive in the market. Pricing strategies can vary based on experience, project complexity, and market demand. This chapter explores effective approaches to pricing your AI services and navigating negotiations with clients.

Understanding Your Value

- **Assess Your Skill Level**: Consider your proficiency in AI, including your technical skills, project experience, and any unique expertise you bring to the table. Higher expertise can command higher rates.
- **Market Rates**: Research the going rates for similar AI freelance services. Platforms like Upwork, Glassdoor, and Payscale can provide insights into industry standards.
- **Value Proposition**: Consider the value your work brings to clients. Projects that significantly enhance a client's operations, sales, or customer satisfaction might warrant higher pricing.

Pricing Models for AI Services

- **Hourly Rate**: Charging by the hour is common for freelance work, especially for projects with undefined scopes or ongoing maintenance work. Ensure your hourly rate reflects your expertise and the complexity of AI tasks.

- **Project-Based Pricing**: For projects with a clear scope and deliverables, a flat fee can be more appropriate. This requires a thorough understanding of the project requirements and your own work process to avoid underestimating the effort involved.
- **Retainer Model**: For ongoing work, a retainer model ensures a fixed monthly income and provides the client with a set number of hours or deliverables each month. This model is ideal for long-term collaborations.
- **Value-Based Pricing**: This involves setting your fees based on the value the project brings to the client. For high-impact AI projects, this can result in significantly higher rates but requires a strong understanding of the client's business and clear communication of the projected ROI.

Setting Your Rates

- **Calculate Your Baseline**: Determine your minimum acceptable rate based on your living expenses, business costs, and desired profit margin. This ensures your rates cover your financial needs.
- **Factor in Indirect Work**: Consider the time spent on non-billable tasks like administration, marketing, and professional development when setting your rates.
- **Adjust for Specialization**: If you specialize in a niche AI area with high demand but few experts, you can charge a premium for your specialized skills.

Communicating Your Rates

- **Transparency**: Be clear and upfront about your pricing structure. Provide detailed proposals that outline the scope of work, deliverables, timelines, and costs.
- **Negotiation**: Be open to negotiation, but know your worth and the minimum rate you're willing to accept. Highlight the value and expertise you bring to the project during negotiations.
- **Flexible Pricing Strategies**: Consider offering different pricing packages or options to accommodate various client budgets while ensuring fair compensation for your work.

Conclusion

Pricing your AI freelance services involves a careful balance between understanding your market value, assessing client needs and project complexities, and clearly communicating your pricing structure. By adopting a strategic approach to pricing, you can ensure fair compensation for your expertise while building sustainable client relationships.

6.1 Understanding Your Value

As an AI freelancer, recognizing and articulating your value is pivotal in setting appropriate rates and securing projects that reflect your worth. Your value encompasses not only your technical skills but also your experience, problem-solving abilities, and the unique perspectives you bring to AI projects. Here's how to assess and communicate your value effectively.

Assess Your Technical Expertise

- **Skill Set**: Evaluate the depth and breadth of your AI skills. Are you proficient in cutting-edge technologies and methodologies? Do you have certifications or formal education in AI-related fields?
- **Specialization**: Consider if you specialize in a niche within AI, such as deep learning, natural language processing, or computer vision. Specialization in a high-demand area can significantly increase your value.
- **Portfolio**: Review your portfolio of completed projects. Successful implementations that demonstrate your ability to solve complex problems can justify higher rates.

Consider Your Experience

- **Industry Experience**: Have you worked in specific industries where AI applications are critical? Experience in sectors like healthcare, finance, or e-commerce can enhance your value to clients in those fields.
- **Project Complexity**: Reflect on the complexity of projects you've tackled. Projects that required innovative solutions or involved high-stakes outcomes showcase your ability to handle challenging work.
- **Client Testimonials**: Positive feedback from past clients can be a strong indicator of your reliability, professionalism, and the quality of your work.

Recognize Your Soft Skills

- **Problem-Solving**: Your ability to approach problems creatively and come up with effective solutions is invaluable. Highlight instances where your innovative thinking led to successful outcomes.
- **Communication**: Effective communication, especially the ability to translate complex AI concepts into understandable terms for non-technical clients, adds significant value.
- **Project Management**: Skills in managing projects, meeting deadlines, and coordinating with teams or stakeholders contribute to your overall value as a freelancer.

Evaluate the Market Demand

- **Demand for Skills**: Research the current demand for your specific AI skills. High demand coupled with a limited supply of experts in your niche can increase your market value.
- **Industry Trends**: Stay informed about emerging trends in AI and how they impact various industries. Being ahead in applying new technologies or methodologies can set you apart.

Articulate Your Value Proposition

Once you've assessed your value, the next step is to articulate it effectively to potential clients. This involves:

- **Clear Communication**: Be clear about what you offer and how it benefits the client. Use concrete examples from your past work to illustrate your points.
- **Confidence**: Present your skills and experiences confidently. Believe in your value, and clients are more likely to recognize it as well.
- **Customization**: Tailor your value proposition for each client or project, focusing on how your specific skills and experiences align with their needs.

Conclusion

Understanding and communicating your value as an AI freelancer involves a comprehensive assessment of your technical skills, experience, soft skills, and market demand. By confidently articulating your unique value proposition, you can set competitive rates and attract projects that are a good fit for your expertise, ultimately leading to a more fulfilling and profitable freelance career.

6.2 Setting Rates and Negotiating Prices

Setting competitive yet fair rates is crucial for AI freelancers, as it directly impacts your earning potential and market positioning. Moreover, negotiating prices with clients requires a balance between valuing your services and understanding client budgets. Here's a guide to establishing your rates and navigating price negotiations effectively.

Establishing Your Rates

- **Assess Your Costs**: Consider your operational costs, including software subscriptions, hardware, continued education, and taxes. Your rates should cover these expenses while ensuring a profit margin.
- **Market Research**: Investigate the going rates for AI services similar to yours. This can vary widely depending on factors like specialization, project complexity, and geographical location.
- **Experience and Expertise**: Higher experience and specialized expertise typically command higher rates. Reflect on your qualifications, portfolio, and the unique value you bring to projects.
- **Rate Models**: Decide whether an hourly, project-based, or retainer model suits your working style and the types of projects you undertake. Each has its advantages depending on the project scope and duration.

Communicating Your Rates

- **Transparency**: Be upfront about your rates in your initial discussions. Clear communication helps set expectations and reduces the likelihood of misunderstandings later on.
- **Justification**: Be prepared to explain how you arrived at your rates, emphasizing the value and results you deliver. Referencing past successful projects can be persuasive.
- **Flexibility**: While it's important to value your work appropriately, be open to negotiation within reason,

especially if a project offers strategic value or long-term
collaboration potential.

Negotiating with Clients

- **Understand Client Budgets**: Start by understanding
  the client's budget and project requirements. This can
  help you tailor your services to fit their financial
  constraints without undervaluing your work.
- **Value Proposition**: Focus negotiations on the value
  you bring rather than just the cost. Highlight how your
  AI expertise can solve their problems, improve
  efficiency, or increase revenue.
- **Alternative Solutions**: If a client's budget is
  significantly lower than your rates, consider offering
  scaled-down services or a phased project approach that
  fits their budget while still providing value.
- **Written Agreements**: Once you've agreed on rates,
  ensure all terms are clearly outlined in a written
  contract. This should include payment terms, project
  scope, deliverables, and any other relevant details.

Handling Rate Pushback

- **Be Prepared**: Some clients may push back on rates.
  Have a rationale ready, explaining the factors that
  influence your pricing, such as the complexity of AI
  projects, the specialized skills required, and the
  potential ROI for the client.
- **Negotiation Limits**: Set clear boundaries for how low
  you're willing to go. Consider non-monetary benefits

like exposure, networking opportunities, or future work when deciding on these limits.

- **Walk Away When Necessary**: If a client's budget is too far below your minimum rate or if they undervalue your services, be prepared to walk away from the negotiation. Engaging in work that significantly undervalues your expertise can set a precedent and impact your market positioning.

Conclusion

Setting and negotiating rates is a critical aspect of freelancing that directly affects your livelihood. By thoroughly understanding your value, researching the market, and communicating effectively, you can set fair rates that reflect your expertise. Successful negotiation is about finding a win-win solution that respects your worth and meets client needs, ensuring a fruitful and lasting professional relationship.

6.3 Handling Financial Transactions Securely

For AI freelancers, managing financial transactions securely is paramount to maintaining trust with clients and ensuring the stability of your freelance business. Given the digital nature of freelance work, especially in the AI field, it's crucial to adopt secure and efficient methods for invoicing, receiving payments, and managing finances. Here's a guide to handling financial transactions securely.

Choosing Secure Payment Platforms

- **Reputable Platforms**: Utilize well-known payment platforms like PayPal, Stripe, or TransferWise for invoicing and receiving payments. These platforms provide secure transaction processing and protection against unauthorized transactions.
- **Bank Transfers**: For larger payments, consider direct bank transfers, which can be more cost-effective. Ensure you're using secure banking portals and that both parties understand any transaction fees involved.

Creating Professional Invoices

- **Invoicing Software**: Use reputable invoicing software that not only helps create professional and clear invoices but also offers secure storage of client information and payment tracking. Tools like FreshBooks, QuickBooks, and Zoho Invoice are popular choices.
- **Detailed Invoices**: Ensure your invoices clearly outline the services provided, rates, total amount due, payment terms (such as due dates), and accepted payment methods. This clarity helps avoid misunderstandings and delays.

Establishing Clear Payment Terms

- **Upfront Agreements**: Discuss and agree on payment terms before starting a project, including rates, payment schedule (e.g., upfront deposits, milestones), and late payment policies. Include these terms in your contract.

- **Deposits and Milestones**: For larger projects, consider requiring an upfront deposit or setting up milestone payments. This approach not only secures part of your payment upfront but also aligns payment with project progress, reducing risk.

Protecting Your Financial Information

- **Secure Connections**: Always access payment platforms and banking portals via secure, private connections. Avoid conducting financial transactions over public Wi-Fi networks.
- **Two-Factor Authentication (2FA)**: Enable 2FA on all financial accounts to add an extra layer of security. This requires a second form of verification, such as a code sent to your phone, in addition to your password.
- **Regular Monitoring**: Regularly review your financial accounts for any unauthorized or suspicious transactions. Promptly report any anomalies to your bank or payment platform.

Handling Late Payments

- **Reminder System**: Set up a system for tracking invoice due dates and sending polite reminder emails for overdue payments. Many invoicing tools offer automated reminder features.
- **Communication**: If a payment is significantly overdue, reach out to the client directly to understand the

situation. Maintain professionalism and seek to find a resolution.

- **Legal Recourse**: For persistently unpaid invoices, consider legal recourse as a last resort. Small claims court or mediation can be options, depending on the amount and your jurisdiction.

Financial Management Best Practices

- **Separate Business and Personal Accounts**: Keep your business finances separate from your personal accounts to simplify accounting and tax filing.
- **Regular Financial Review**: Schedule regular reviews of your financial status, including income, expenses, and cash flow, to ensure the health of your freelance business.
- **Save for Taxes**: Set aside a portion of each payment for taxes. Consider working with a financial advisor or accountant to understand your tax obligations and plan accordingly.

Conclusion

Securing financial transactions is a critical aspect of freelancing, ensuring that you're compensated for your work and that your business operates smoothly. By adopting secure payment methods, setting clear payment terms, and managing your finances diligently, you can minimize risks and maintain a healthy, trustworthy freelance operation.

Chapter 7: Scaling Your AI Freelance Business

Scaling your AI freelance business means expanding your client base, increasing revenue, and potentially growing your service offerings. As the demand for AI expertise continues to rise, there are strategic ways to scale your operations without compromising the quality of your work or your work-life balance. Here's a guide to effectively scaling your AI freelance business.

Diversify Your Service Offerings

- **Explore New AI Domains**: Stay abreast of emerging AI technologies and consider expanding your services to include these new areas. This could involve branching into fields like reinforcement learning, generative adversarial networks (GANs), or AI ethics consulting.
- **Package Services**: Create service packages that combine various aspects of your work, such as data cleaning, model development, and deployment, offering a comprehensive solution to clients.

Build a Strong Online Presence

- **Content Marketing**: Share your expertise through blogs, webinars, or tutorials. High-quality content can attract potential clients and establish you as a thought leader in the AI space.

- **Social Media Engagement**: Actively engage on platforms like LinkedIn and Twitter, sharing insights, joining discussions, and connecting with other professionals in the AI field.

Leverage Client Referrals and Testimonials

- **Referral Programs**: Encourage satisfied clients to refer new clients by offering incentives, such as discounts on future services. Word-of-mouth remains a powerful tool for business growth.
- **Showcase Success Stories**: Use client testimonials and case studies on your website and in your pitches to demonstrate the impact of your work and build credibility with prospective clients.

Automate and Delegate Non-Core Tasks

- **Use AI Tools**: Leverage AI and automation tools for administrative tasks like scheduling, invoicing, and email management, freeing up more time for billable work.
- **Outsource**: Consider outsourcing tasks outside your expertise, such as graphic design, marketing, or accounting. This allows you to focus on your core AI services.

Collaborate and Expand Your Team

- **Collaboration**: Partner with other freelancers or agencies on larger projects. This can help you tackle bigger projects than you could manage alone and open up new client opportunities.

- **Hiring**: As your business grows, hiring part-time or contract professionals, such as junior data scientists or project managers, can help manage the increased workload.

Strengthen Client Relationships

- **Regular Check-ins**: Schedule regular meetings with clients to discuss ongoing projects, future needs, and potential improvements. Strong relationships can lead to repeat business and referrals.
- **Exceed Expectations**: Consistently deliver high-quality work and look for ways to add value to your client engagements. Satisfied clients are more likely to offer larger projects and refer you to others.

Invest in Continuous Learning

- **Stay Updated**: AI is a rapidly evolving field. Regularly update your skills and knowledge to offer the latest solutions to your clients. This can involve taking advanced courses, attending conferences, and participating in relevant workshops.

Financial Management for Growth

- **Reinvest in Your Business**: Allocate a portion of your profits towards business growth activities, such as marketing, professional development, or technology upgrades.

- **Financial Planning**: Work with a financial advisor to manage increased revenue, plan for taxes efficiently, and set financial goals for your business.

Conclusion

Scaling your AI freelance business involves a combination of expanding your services, leveraging technology for efficiency, building strong client relationships, and continuously improving your skills. By strategically planning for growth and investing in your business, you can achieve sustainable expansion while maintaining the quality and integrity of your services.

7.1 Growing Your Client Base

Expanding your client base is essential for scaling your AI freelance business and ensuring a steady stream of projects. Achieving this growth involves not only showcasing your expertise and delivering exceptional work but also adopting strategic marketing and networking efforts. Here are effective strategies to attract new clients and grow your AI freelance business.

Leverage Your Network

- **Referrals**: Encourage satisfied clients to refer you to their peers by providing outstanding service. Consider offering a referral incentive to motivate clients to recommend your services.
- **Professional Networks**: Engage with your existing professional network, including former colleagues,

classmates, and industry contacts. Let them know about your freelance business and the services you offer.

Optimize Your Online Presence

- **Professional Website**: Ensure your website is professional, up-to-date, and showcases your portfolio, testimonials, and the range of AI services you offer. SEO optimization can help potential clients find you more easily.
- **Social Media**: Use platforms like LinkedIn and Twitter to share insights, comment on industry trends, and participate in relevant discussions. This can increase your visibility and attract clients interested in AI solutions.

Content Marketing

- **Blogging**: Write blog posts that highlight your expertise in AI, discuss case studies, or explain complex AI concepts in layman's terms. This can establish you as a thought leader and attract clients looking for knowledgeable freelancers.
- **Webinars and Workshops**: Host webinars or workshops on AI topics. This not only showcases your expertise but also directly engages potential clients who are interested in AI solutions.

Specialize in a Niche

- **Identify a Niche**: Specializing in a specific AI niche, such as healthcare, finance, or retail, can make you the go-to expert for clients in these industries. Deep knowledge of an industry's challenges and regulations can set you apart from generalists.

- **Tailored Solutions**: Develop and market AI solutions tailored to your niche's specific needs. Demonstrating a deep understanding of these needs can attract clients looking for specialized expertise.

Participate in AI Competitions and Hackathons

- **Showcase Your Skills**: Participating in competitions like those hosted on Kaggle or in hackathons can not only hone your skills but also showcase your expertise to a broader audience, including potential clients and collaborators.
- **Networking**: These events offer excellent networking opportunities. Engage with fellow participants, share your experiences, and discuss potential collaboration opportunities.

Collaborate with Agencies and Other Freelancers

- **Partnerships**: Establish partnerships with agencies or other freelancers who offer complementary services. For example, if you specialize in AI model development, you could partner with a data engineering freelancer or agency.
- **Referral Agreements**: Set up referral agreements with your partners, where you refer clients to each other based on the project's needs. This can be a mutually beneficial way to expand your client base.

Offer Free Initial Consultations

- **Build Trust**: Offering a free initial consultation can help build trust with potential clients. It provides an opportunity to understand their needs, offer preliminary insights, and demonstrate your expertise without any commitment from the client.
- **Value Proposition**: Use the consultation to articulate the value your AI services can bring to their business, tailoring your approach to their specific challenges and goals.

Conclusion

Growing your AI freelance client base requires a combination of showcasing your expertise, strategic networking, and targeted marketing efforts. By focusing on building strong relationships, delivering value, and positioning yourself as an expert in your field, you can attract new clients and sustainably scale your freelance business.

7.2 Outsourcing and Team Building

As your AI freelance business grows, you may find that the demand for your services exceeds your capacity to deliver solo. Outsourcing tasks or building a team can help you manage this increased workload, allowing you to take on more projects and diversify your offerings. Here's how to approach outsourcing and team building effectively.

Identifying Tasks to Outsource

- **Non-Core Tasks**: Identify tasks that are necessary for your business but fall outside your core AI expertise, such as administrative duties, graphic design, or content writing. Outsourcing these tasks can free up your time to focus on high-value AI work.
- **Specialized Skills**: For projects that require expertise beyond your skill set, consider outsourcing to specialists. For example, if a project requires advanced front-end development alongside AI, partnering with a freelance developer can enhance the project's quality.

Finding the Right Talent

- **Freelance Platforms**: Platforms like Upwork, Toptal, and Freelancer can be great sources to find skilled professionals for outsourcing. Look for freelancers with strong portfolios and positive reviews.
- **Professional Networks**: Tap into your professional network for recommendations. Often, the best talent comes through referrals from trusted colleagues and peers.
- **AI Communities**: Engage with AI and tech communities online and at conferences. These can be great places to meet potential collaborators who share your passion for AI.

Building a Collaborative Team

- **Shared Vision**: When building a team, ensure that everyone shares a common vision and understanding of the project goals. This alignment is crucial for cohesive and efficient collaboration.

- **Clear Communication**: Establish clear channels of communication and regular check-ins to keep everyone aligned. Tools like Slack, Trello, and Zoom can facilitate effective team collaboration.
- **Defined Roles and Responsibilities**: Clearly define each team member's role and responsibilities to avoid overlaps and ensure all aspects of the project are covered.

Managing Outsourced Work

- **Contracts and Agreements**: Ensure there are clear contracts in place with freelancers or contractors that outline the scope of work, deliverables, timelines, and payment terms.
- **Quality Control**: Implement a quality control process to ensure that outsourced work meets your standards and the client's expectations. This might involve regular reviews and feedback loops.
- **Building Relationships**: Treat your freelancers and contractors as valued team members. Building positive relationships can lead to long-term collaborations.

Scaling Responsibly

- **Gradual Growth**: Scale your team gradually to manage the increased complexity and ensure you can maintain a steady flow of projects to support the larger team.
- **Financial Planning**: Consider the financial implications of outsourcing and team building, including the costs

of hiring and the potential need for increased project management and coordination efforts.

- **Flexibility**: Maintain flexibility in your team structure to adapt to the fluctuating demands of freelance work. A mix of permanent team members and freelancers can offer both stability and flexibility.

Conclusion

Outsourcing and team building can significantly enhance your capacity to deliver AI projects, allowing you to scale your freelance business. By carefully selecting the right tasks to outsource, finding skilled professionals, and fostering a collaborative team environment, you can handle a larger volume and variety of projects while maintaining high-quality standards.

7.3 Creating Passive Income Streams

For AI freelancers, diversifying income sources can provide financial stability and reduce reliance on active project work. Creating passive income streams allows you to earn revenue even when you're not actively working on client projects. Here are some strategies for AI freelancers to develop passive income streams.

Develop AI Tools or Products

- **Software Tools**: Develop and sell AI-powered tools or software applications that cater to common needs in your industry, such as data analysis tools, chatbots, or automation scripts.

- **Pre-built Models**: Create and sell pre-trained AI models that other developers or businesses can integrate into their applications, saving them time and resources.

Create Educational Content

- **Online Courses and Tutorials**: Leverage your AI expertise to create and sell online courses or tutorials on platforms like Udemy, Coursera, or your website. Topics can range from introductory AI concepts to advanced techniques in machine learning, NLP, or computer vision.
- **E-books and Guides**: Write and publish e-books or comprehensive guides on AI topics. These can be sold on platforms like Amazon Kindle Direct Publishing or your website.

Monetize Your Blog or YouTube Channel

- **Ad Revenue**: If you run a blog or YouTube channel where you share AI insights, tutorials, or project case studies, consider monetizing through ad revenue once you've built a significant audience.
- **Affiliate Marketing**: Recommend AI tools, books, or courses using affiliate links. You'll earn a commission for purchases made through your links, providing a passive income stream.

Offer Paid Subscriptions

- **Membership Site**: Create a membership site or a Patreon account where subscribers pay for exclusive content, such as in-depth articles, video content, or early access to your tools and applications.
- **Newsletter**: Launch a subscription-based newsletter offering AI industry insights, trends, and analysis, providing value to professionals and enthusiasts willing to pay for high-quality information.

Licensing and Royalties

- **Licensing Your Work**: License your AI models, algorithms, or software to companies or other freelancers. This arrangement can provide a steady income stream through licensing fees.
- **Stock Photography and Art**: If you work with AI-generated art or photography, consider selling your creations on stock photo websites or art platforms, earning royalties for each download or purchase.

Crowdsourcing and Donations

- **Open-Source Contributions**: If you contribute to open-source AI projects, consider setting up a GitHub Sponsors account or a Buy Me a Coffee page to receive donations from those who find value in your work.

Considerations for Passive Income

- **Time Investment**: Developing passive income streams often requires a significant upfront time investment. Balance this with your active client work to avoid burnout.
- **Market Need**: Research and validate the market need for your passive income idea to ensure there's a demand for what you plan to offer.
- **Continuous Promotion**: Passive income streams typically require ongoing marketing efforts to maintain and grow revenue over time.

Conclusion

Creating passive income streams can provide AI freelancers with financial security and the freedom to pursue projects they're passionate about. By leveraging your AI expertise to develop products, content, or services that offer ongoing value, you can build a diversified income portfolio that supports your freelance career in the long term.

Chapter 8: Legal and Ethical Considerations

As AI technology continues to advance, legal and ethical considerations become increasingly important for freelancers working in this space. Ensuring compliance with laws and maintaining high ethical standards not only protects your freelance business but also builds trust with your clients. Here are key legal and ethical considerations for AI freelancers.

Legal Considerations

- **Contracts and Agreements**: Always formalize client engagements with a contract that clearly outlines project scope, deliverables, timelines, payment terms, and confidentiality obligations. This protects both parties in case of disputes.
- **Intellectual Property Rights**: Understand the intellectual property (IP) implications of your work. Clarify ownership of the AI models, algorithms, and any data used or generated during a project. Include IP terms in your contracts.
- **Data Privacy and Protection**: With AI projects often involving large datasets, be aware of data privacy laws such as GDPR in the EU or CCPA in California. Ensure compliance with data handling, storage, and processing regulations.
- **Liability and Indemnification**: Define liability terms in your contracts, particularly for projects where AI decisions could have significant consequences.

Consider professional liability insurance to protect against potential claims.

Ethical Considerations

- **Transparency**: Be transparent with clients about the capabilities and limitations of AI solutions. Set realistic expectations to avoid misunderstandings about what AI can and cannot achieve.
- **Bias and Fairness**: AI systems can inadvertently perpetuate or amplify biases present in training data. Strive to use diverse and representative datasets, and test your models for bias. Discuss potential bias issues with clients and work towards fair and equitable AI solutions.
- **Accountability**: Take responsibility for the AI solutions you develop. If an AI system could make decisions impacting individuals' lives or livelihoods, ensure there are mechanisms for accountability and redress.
- **Sustainability**: Consider the environmental impact of training and running AI models, particularly large models that require significant computational resources. Explore ways to optimize model efficiency and reduce carbon footprint.

Navigating Ethical Dilemmas

- **Stay Informed**: Keep abreast of emerging ethical guidelines and frameworks in the AI field. Organizations like the IEEE and the ACM offer resources and guidelines on ethical AI development.

- **Professional Judgment**: Use your professional judgment to navigate ethical dilemmas. When in doubt, consider consulting with peers or seeking advice from industry ethics boards.
- **Client Education**: Educate your clients about the ethical implications of AI projects. Encourage the adoption of ethical AI practices in project planning and execution.

Conclusion

For AI freelancers, navigating legal and ethical considerations is crucial for maintaining a reputable and responsible practice. By adhering to legal requirements, upholding ethical standards, and transparently communicating with clients, you can contribute to the development of AI solutions that are not only innovative but also ethical and socially responsible.

8.1 Contracts and Agreements

For AI freelancers, having well-structured contracts and agreements in place is essential for defining the scope of work, protecting intellectual property, and ensuring clear communication between you and your clients. A comprehensive contract not only provides legal protection but also sets the foundation for a successful and professional working relationship. Here's how to approach contracts and agreements in AI freelance projects.

Key Elements of AI Freelance Contracts

- **Scope of Work**: Clearly define the project scope, including the AI services to be provided, project milestones, deliverables, and deadlines. This helps prevent scope creep and ensures both parties have a mutual understanding of the project expectations.
- **Payment Terms**: Outline the payment structure, including rates (hourly, project-based, or retainer), payment schedules, invoicing procedures, and any upfront deposits required. Include late payment policies to encourage timely payments.
- **Intellectual Property (IP) Rights**: Specify the ownership of the IP related to the project. This includes the AI models, algorithms, code, and any data generated during the project. Clarify whether the IP will be owned by the client, remain with you, or if a licensing agreement is in place.
- **Confidentiality and Data Protection**: Include confidentiality clauses to protect sensitive information shared during the project. Address how data will be handled, stored, and protected, especially if dealing with personal or sensitive data subject to regulations like GDPR.
- **Liability and Indemnification**: Define the liability limitations for each party, particularly for projects where AI decisions could have significant consequences. Consider including an indemnification clause to protect against third-party claims related to the project work.

- **Termination Clause**: Outline the conditions under which the contract can be terminated by either party. Include notice periods and any financial settlements required upon termination.
- **Dispute Resolution**: Specify the process for resolving any disputes that may arise, including the jurisdiction and legal framework that will govern the contract.

Best Practices for AI Freelance Contracts

- **Use Plain Language**: Write contracts in clear, straightforward language to ensure both parties fully understand the terms and conditions.
- **Customize for Each Project**: While you may have a standard contract template, tailor each contract to the specific project and client to address unique requirements and risks.
- **Review and Negotiation**: Be open to reviewing and negotiating contract terms with your client. This collaborative approach can lead to a fair agreement that meets both parties' needs.
- **Legal Review**: Consider having your contract templates reviewed by a legal professional, especially if you work on complex AI projects or with clients in different jurisdictions.
- **Record Keeping**: Keep signed copies of all contracts and agreements for your records. Digital contract management tools can help organize and store your documents securely.

Conclusion

Contracts and agreements are foundational to a successful freelance practice, providing a clear framework for your AI projects and safeguarding your interests. By ensuring your contracts are comprehensive, clear, and tailored to each project, you can foster positive client relationships and mitigate potential legal risks.

8.2 Intellectual Property Rights

Intellectual property (IP) rights are a critical consideration for AI freelancers, as the nature of AI work often involves the creation, use, and manipulation of proprietary algorithms, models, and data. Understanding and clearly defining IP rights in your freelance contracts not only protects your creations but also clarifies ownership and usage rights for your clients. Here's what you need to know about handling IP rights in AI freelance projects.

Understanding IP in AI Projects

- **Types of IP**: AI projects can involve various types of IP, including software code, algorithms, machine learning models, datasets, and even the generated outputs. Each type of IP may require different considerations and protections.
- **Ownership**: IP ownership can be a complex issue in AI projects. It's essential to determine who owns the IP created during a project—the freelancer, the client, or both. This can depend on factors like the nature of the

work, the source of the data used, and the terms agreed upon in the contract.

Clarifying IP Rights in Contracts

- **Explicit Terms**: Clearly outline IP ownership terms in your contracts. Specify whether the IP developed during the project will be owned by the client, retained by you, or if a licensing agreement will be established for the client to use the IP.
- **Licensing**: If opting for a licensing agreement, detail the scope of the license (exclusive or non-exclusive), the duration, and any specific usage rights or restrictions. This allows you to retain ownership while granting the client the rights to use the IP for their purposes.
- **Pre-existing IP**: If the project involves using pre-existing IP (yours or third-party), clarify how this IP will be treated. Ensure you have the right to use any third-party IP and outline any limitations on the client's use of this IP.
- **Contributions and Collaborations**: For projects involving collaboration with other freelancers or the client's in-house team, specify how contributions to the IP will be handled and attributed.

Protecting Your IP

- **Non-Disclosure Agreements (NDAs)**: Consider using NDAs to protect the confidentiality of your proprietary methods, algorithms, or data, especially during initial client discussions.

- **Documentation**: Keep thorough documentation of your development process, including design decisions, data sources, and version control. This can serve as evidence of your IP ownership if disputes arise.
- **IP Registration**: In some cases, it may be beneficial to register your IP (e.g., patents for unique algorithms or trademarks for software names). Consult with an IP attorney to understand the best approach for your work.

Navigating IP Challenges

- **Data Rights**: AI projects often require large datasets for training models. Ensure you have the rights to use any data provided by the client and clarify the ownership of any data generated during the project.
- **Open Source Considerations**: If your work involves open-source tools or libraries, ensure you comply with their licenses and clearly communicate any implications for the project's IP.
- **International Projects**: For projects with international clients, be aware of the IP laws in the client's country, as they can differ significantly from your own. Tailor your contracts accordingly.

Conclusion

Effectively managing IP rights is crucial for AI freelancers to protect their creations and ensure clear agreements with clients. By incorporating comprehensive IP terms in your contracts and taking steps to safeguard your IP, you can navigate the complexities of IP ownership in AI projects, fostering trust and transparency with your clients.

8.3 Ethical AI Practices

In the rapidly evolving field of artificial intelligence, ethical considerations play a crucial role in guiding the development and deployment of AI systems. As an AI freelancer, adhering to ethical AI practices not only ensures the responsible use of technology but also builds trust with clients and end-users. Here's how to incorporate ethical considerations into your AI projects.

Transparency and Explainability

- **Clear Communication**: Be transparent with clients about how AI systems make decisions, the data they use, and their capabilities and limitations. Avoid overpromising or creating unrealistic expectations about what AI can achieve.
- **Explainable AI**: Whenever possible, utilize or develop AI models that are explainable and understandable by non-experts. This is particularly important for projects in sensitive areas like healthcare, finance, or legal, where decisions need to be interpretable.

Fairness and Bias Mitigation

- **Diverse Data Sets**: Ensure the data used for training AI models is diverse and representative to prevent biases. Biased data can lead to skewed outcomes that may unintentionally discriminate against certain groups.

- **Bias Testing**: Regularly test your AI models for bias. Tools and frameworks are available to help identify and mitigate bias in AI systems. Make adjustments as necessary to ensure fairness.

Privacy and Data Security

- **Data Protection**: Implement strong data protection measures to safeguard personal and sensitive information. Follow best practices for data encryption, secure data storage, and secure data transfer.
- **Compliance**: Stay informed about and comply with relevant data protection regulations, such as GDPR in Europe or CCPA in California, which set standards for privacy and data protection.

Accountability and Responsibility

- **Clear Accountability**: Establish clear lines of accountability for AI decision-making. Ensure there is always a human in the loop, particularly for critical decisions, to provide oversight and the ability to intervene if necessary.
- **Impact Assessment**: Before deploying AI solutions, assess their potential impact on individuals and society. Consider the ethical implications and strive to minimize negative outcomes.

Sustainable AI Practices

- **Energy Efficiency**: Be mindful of the environmental impact of training and deploying AI models. Opt for more energy-efficient algorithms and practices where possible, and consider the carbon footprint of your computing resources.

Promoting Ethical AI

- **Client Education**: Educate your clients about the importance of ethical AI practices. Advocate for ethical considerations to be integrated into project planning and execution from the outset.
- **Continuous Learning**: Stay informed about the latest developments in ethical AI, including emerging guidelines, frameworks, and tools designed to promote responsible AI development.

Ethical Dilemmas

- **Seek Guidance**: When faced with ethical dilemmas, seek guidance from peers, industry experts, or ethics boards. Engage in professional forums or communities dedicated to ethical AI to share experiences and seek advice.

Conclusion

Integrating ethical considerations into your AI freelance work is essential for ensuring the responsible development and use of AI technologies. By prioritizing transparency, fairness, privacy, and accountability, you can contribute to the development of AI solutions that are not only innovative but also ethical and beneficial to society.

Chapter 9: Future of AI in Freelancing

The intersection of AI and freelancing is a dynamic landscape, continuously shaped by technological advancements, market demands, and evolving work paradigms. As we look towards the future, several trends and opportunities are emerging that AI freelancers should be aware of to stay ahead in the field. Here's an exploration of what the future holds for AI in freelancing.

Continued Expansion of AI Applications

- **Broader Integration**: AI will continue to be integrated into a wide array of industries, from healthcare and education to marketing and entertainment, expanding the demand for AI expertise.
- **Innovative Solutions**: The development of new AI technologies and methodologies will open up novel applications and services that freelancers can offer, such as generative AI for content creation, AI-driven personalization engines, and advanced predictive analytics.

Emergence of New Specializations

- **Ethical AI Consulting**: As awareness of the ethical implications of AI grows, there will be a higher demand for specialists who can guide companies in developing responsible AI solutions.

- **AI Governance**: Experts in AI governance and regulation will be needed to help organizations navigate the complex legal landscape surrounding AI, ensuring compliance and ethical use.

Impact of AI on Freelancing Itself

- **Automation of Freelance Tasks**: AI tools will increasingly automate administrative and routine tasks for freelancers, from scheduling and communication to invoicing and market analysis, allowing more focus on high-value creative work.
- **AI Collaboration Tools**: Advanced AI collaboration tools will facilitate more efficient remote work and project management, enabling freelancers to work more seamlessly with clients and teams across the globe.

Upskilling and Continuous Learning

- **Lifelong Learning**: The fast pace of AI development will necessitate continuous upskilling and adaptation. Freelancers will need to stay abreast of the latest AI advancements, tools, and best practices to remain competitive.
- **Cross-Disciplinary Skills**: The convergence of AI with other fields will require freelancers to develop cross-disciplinary skills, blending AI expertise with domain-specific knowledge to offer more comprehensive solutions.

Networking and Community Building

- **Global AI Freelance Communities**: The growth of online platforms and communities will facilitate stronger networks among AI freelancers, offering opportunities for collaboration, knowledge sharing, and mentorship.
- **Hybrid Work Models**: The blending of freelance and traditional work models may lead to hybrid arrangements, where freelancers engage in long-term collaborations with organizations, blurring the lines between freelancing and employment.

Ethical and Societal Considerations

- **Focus on Ethical AI**: There will be a heightened focus on developing AI in an ethical, transparent, and accountable manner, with freelancers playing a crucial role in advocating for and implementing ethical AI practices.
- **AI and Society**: Freelancers will need to consider the broader societal implications of their work, ensuring that AI solutions contribute positively to society and do not exacerbate inequalities or harm.

Conclusion

The future of AI in freelancing is bright, filled with opportunities for growth, innovation, and collaboration. By embracing continuous learning, adapting to new technologies, and upholding ethical standards, AI freelancers can not only thrive in their careers but also contribute to the responsible advancement of AI technology. Staying informed and engaged with the AI community will be key to navigating the exciting developments that lie ahead.

9.1 Emerging Trends and Technologies

The AI landscape is continuously evolving, with new trends and technologies shaping the future of freelancing in this domain. Staying ahead of these developments can position AI freelancers as leaders in their field, ready to meet the demands of tomorrow's projects. Here are some emerging trends and technologies in AI that freelancers should watch.

Generative AI

- **Overview**: Generative AI refers to algorithms that can generate new content, from text and images to music and videos, based on existing data. Tools like GPT-3 for text generation and DALL-E for image creation exemplify this trend.
- **Implications for Freelancers**: As generative AI becomes more sophisticated, opportunities for freelancers in creative fields, content generation, and design will expand. Understanding and leveraging these tools can add a new dimension to your service offerings.

AI in Cybersecurity

- **Overview**: With cyber threats becoming more complex, AI is increasingly used to enhance cybersecurity measures through predictive analytics, threat detection, and automated responses.

- **Implications for Freelancers**: Freelancers specializing in cybersecurity can leverage AI to offer advanced security solutions. Additionally, all freelancers will need to understand AI-based security to protect their own and their clients' data.

Edge AI

- **Overview**: Edge AI involves processing AI algorithms on local devices (edge devices) rather than relying on cloud computing. This approach reduces latency, conserves bandwidth, and enhances privacy.
- **Implications for Freelancers**: Freelancers working in IoT, mobile app development, and wearable technologies will find opportunities in integrating AI capabilities directly into devices, opening up new avenues for innovation.

AI for Sustainability

- **Overview**: AI is being used to tackle environmental challenges, from optimizing energy consumption in smart grids to monitoring deforestation and biodiversity loss.
- **Implications for Freelancers**: Freelancers with an interest in environmental science and sustainability can contribute to green tech projects, using AI to develop solutions that address ecological issues.

Quantum AI

- **Overview**: Quantum AI involves the intersection of quantum computing and AI, promising to solve complex problems much faster than classical computers.
- **Implications for Freelancers**: While still in early stages, quantum AI represents a frontier for research and development. Freelancers with expertise in quantum computing and AI can engage in cutting-edge projects at the intersection of these fields.

AI in Healthcare

- **Overview**: AI applications in healthcare are growing, from diagnostic tools and personalized medicine to operational efficiencies in healthcare systems.
- **Implications for Freelancers**: Freelancers with expertise in AI and a background in healthcare can contribute to transformative projects, improving patient outcomes and healthcare delivery.

AI Ethics and Governance

- **Overview**: As AI becomes more integral to society, ethical considerations and governance frameworks are becoming increasingly important to ensure responsible development and deployment.
- **Implications for Freelancers**: Freelancers can play a role in shaping ethical AI practices, working as consultants on AI ethics, or contributing to the development of governance frameworks.

Conclusion

Emerging trends and technologies in AI offer exciting opportunities for freelancers to expand their skill sets and explore new markets. By staying informed about these developments and understanding their implications, AI freelancers can position themselves at the forefront of innovation, ready to meet the evolving needs of clients across industries.

9.2 Preparing for the Future

As the AI landscape continues to evolve, freelancers in this field must proactively prepare for the future to stay competitive and relevant. Adapting to new technologies, continuously learning, and anticipating market needs are crucial strategies for thriving in the dynamic world of AI freelancing. Here are key ways to prepare for the future of AI in freelancing.

Continuous Learning and Skill Development

- **Stay Informed**: Regularly follow AI research, news, and trends to stay up-to-date with the latest developments in the field. Platforms like arXiv, Google Scholar, and AI-focused newsletters and blogs can be valuable resources.
- **Expand Your Skill Set**: Take online courses, attend workshops, and obtain certifications in emerging AI technologies and methodologies. Platforms like Coursera, Udacity, and edX offer courses designed by industry experts and leading universities.

Building a Versatile Portfolio

- **Diverse Projects**: Work on a variety of AI projects across different industries to build a diverse portfolio. This not only demonstrates your breadth of experience but also showcases your ability to adapt to different challenges and requirements.
- **Showcase Innovations**: Include projects in your portfolio that involve emerging AI technologies or innovative applications of AI. Highlighting your involvement in cutting-edge work can attract clients looking for forward-thinking freelancers.

Networking and Community Engagement

- **Professional Networks**: Actively participate in AI and tech communities, both online and offline. Attend conferences, seminars, and meetups to network with peers, share knowledge, and discover new opportunities.
- **Collaboration**: Seek opportunities to collaborate with other AI professionals, researchers, and industry experts. Collaborative projects can lead to new insights, skill development, and expanded professional networks.

Adapting to New Work Paradigms

- **Remote Work and Global Collaboration**: Embrace remote work tools and practices to collaborate effectively with clients and teams across the globe.

Familiarize yourself with project management and communication tools that facilitate remote work.

- **Hybrid Freelance Models**: Be open to hybrid work arrangements that blend freelance projects with part-time or contract roles. This can provide both stability and flexibility, allowing you to pursue a wider range of opportunities.

Ethical AI Practice

- **Understand Ethical Implications**: Educate yourself on the ethical considerations of AI development and use, including issues related to bias, privacy, and accountability. Incorporate ethical practices into your work to ensure responsible AI solutions.
- **Advocate for Ethical AI**: Use your platform and influence to advocate for ethical AI practices within the freelance community and among clients. Contributing to a culture of ethical AI can enhance your reputation and the trust clients place in you.

Financial Planning and Diversification

- **Financial Stability**: Develop a financial plan that accounts for the ebb and flow of freelance work. Consider creating passive income streams, as discussed in earlier chapters, to provide financial stability.
- **Diversify Income Sources**: Explore different avenues for income, such as consulting, teaching, or product development, in addition to project-based work. This diversification can buffer against market fluctuations and reduce dependency on any single income source.

Conclusion

Preparing for the future as an AI freelancer involves a multifaceted approach that includes continuous learning, portfolio diversification, networking, adapting to new work paradigms, ethical practice, and financial planning. By staying agile, embracing new opportunities, and upholding high standards of professionalism and ethics, AI freelancers can navigate the future landscape with confidence and success.

9.3 Lifelong Learning and Adaptation

In the rapidly evolving field of AI, the principles of lifelong learning and adaptation are not just beneficial but essential for freelancers who wish to remain competitive and innovative. The AI landscape is characterized by constant change, with new technologies, methodologies, and applications emerging regularly. Embracing a mindset of continuous learning and flexibility can prepare AI freelancers for the challenges and opportunities that lie ahead.

Embracing Continuous Learning

- **Stay Updated**: Regularly follow AI advancements through journals, blogs, podcasts, and newsletters. Platforms like arXiv for preprints and Google Scholar for academic research are invaluable for staying abreast of the latest developments.
- **Online Courses and Certifications**: Platforms such as Coursera, Udacity, and edX offer a wide range of courses in AI and related fields. These courses are often

created by experts from leading universities and tech companies, providing high-quality, up-to-date content.
- **Workshops and Webinars**: Participate in workshops and webinars that focus on the latest AI tools and techniques. These sessions not only provide learning opportunities but also allow you to ask questions and interact with experts in the field.

Cultivating a Growth Mindset

- **Embrace Challenges**: View challenges as opportunities to grow and learn rather than obstacles. A growth mindset encourages resilience and creativity, essential traits for navigating the uncertainties of freelance work.
- **Feedback and Reflection**: Actively seek feedback on your work and reflect on your experiences. Constructive feedback can highlight areas for improvement and guide your learning efforts.

Adapting to Change

- **Flexibility**: Be open to changing directions or learning new skills in response to market demands and technological advancements. This flexibility can open up new opportunities and niches within the AI field.
- **Innovation**: Use your knowledge and skills to experiment with new ideas and approaches. Innovation not only enhances your service offerings but also distinguishes you in a competitive market.

Building a Supportive Learning Community

- **Networking**: Engage with other AI professionals through social media, professional networking sites like LinkedIn, and community forums. Networking can lead to collaborative learning opportunities and insights into emerging trends.
- **Mentorship**: Seek mentorship from experienced professionals in the field. Conversely, offer mentorship to those newer to AI freelancing. Mentorship relationships can provide mutual learning opportunities and professional growth.

Applying Learning to Practice

- **Personal Projects**: Apply what you learn to personal projects or open-source contributions. This practical application helps consolidate your knowledge and can lead to innovative solutions that enhance your portfolio.
- **Client Projects**: Incorporate new skills and technologies into your client work where appropriate. This not only improves the quality of your work but also demonstrates your commitment to staying at the forefront of AI advancements.

Conclusion

Lifelong learning and adaptation are key to thriving as an AI freelancer in a field characterized by rapid and continuous change. By committing to ongoing education, embracing a growth mindset, staying flexible in the face of new developments, and actively applying new knowledge, AI freelancers can ensure they remain valuable, innovative, and prepared for the future of freelancing in AI.

Conclusion

In the rapidly evolving landscape of artificial intelligence, the role of AI freelancers has become increasingly pivotal. As we've explored throughout this guide, thriving as an AI freelancer requires a blend of technical expertise, continuous learning, strategic business practices, and a strong ethical foundation. The future of AI freelancing is bright, filled with opportunities for innovation, growth, and significant contributions to various industries.

Key Takeaways

- **Technical Proficiency**: Deep knowledge in AI and related technologies is fundamental. Specializing in niche areas can set you apart in a competitive market.
- **Business Acumen**: Understanding how to navigate contracts, pricing, and client relationships is crucial for building a sustainable freelance business.
- **Ethical Considerations**: Ethical AI practices are not optional but essential. They ensure the responsible development and use of AI technologies.
- **Lifelong Learning**: The field of AI is characterized by rapid advancements. Embracing continuous learning and adaptation is vital for staying relevant and innovative.
- **Networking and Community**: Building a professional network and engaging with the AI community can lead to new opportunities, collaborations, and support.

- **Diversification**: Creating passive income streams and diversifying your service offerings can provide financial stability and open up new business avenues.

Looking Ahead

The integration of AI across industries continues to expand, creating a growing demand for skilled AI professionals. Freelancers who can navigate this landscape effectively, combining technical skills with strategic business practices and a commitment to ethical standards, are well-positioned to succeed.

Embracing the Future

As AI freelancers, we have the opportunity to shape the future of this technology. By staying informed, continuously improving our skills, and adhering to ethical standards, we can contribute to the development of AI solutions that are not only innovative but also beneficial to society.

This guide has aimed to provide you with the insights and strategies needed to navigate the world of AI freelancing successfully. The journey ahead is one of exploration, learning, and growth. Embrace it with enthusiasm, and you'll find a rewarding career path that not only meets your professional aspirations but also contributes to the broader field of artificial intelligence.

Your Path Forward in AI Freelancing

Embarking on a journey within the realm of AI freelancing opens a gateway to a world rich with opportunities for innovation, personal growth, and making a tangible impact. As you chart this course, it's crucial to remember that your journey is distinctly yours, shaped by your unique passions, skills, and the choices you make along the way.

Cultivating a Learning Mindset

The cornerstone of a successful AI freelancing career is a commitment to lifelong learning. The AI landscape is in a state of constant flux, with new technologies, methodologies, and applications emerging at a rapid pace. Prioritize continuous education through online platforms, workshops, and self-directed projects to ensure you remain at the forefront of AI advancements.

Specializing While Staying Adaptable

While carving out a niche can set you apart in a crowded field, maintaining adaptability allows you to navigate the shifting sands of technological advancements and market demands. Strive for a balance between deep expertise in your chosen specialization and a broad understanding of the AI spectrum.

Building a Robust Portfolio

Your portfolio is the window through which potential clients view your capabilities. It should be a living document, regularly updated with projects that not only showcase your technical prowess but also your problem-solving acumen. Include detailed case studies that illuminate your process, the challenges you've surmounted, and the tangible benefits your solutions have delivered.

Fostering Professional Relationships

The value of networking in the freelancing landscape cannot be overstated. Engage actively with both the AI and freelancing communities through various channels, from social media to professional networking events. These interactions can lead to fruitful collaborations, referrals, and a deeper understanding of the AI field.

Emphasizing Ethical AI Development

As AI becomes more intertwined with daily life and business operations, the imperative for ethical development practices grows. Uphold principles of transparency, fairness, privacy, and accountability in your projects. This commitment not only serves the greater good but also enhances your standing as a trustworthy and conscientious freelancer.

Optimizing Business Operations

Efficiency in your business processes is key to maximizing your productive output. Employ a suite of digital tools to streamline project management, financial tracking, and client communications. This technological leverage can afford you more time for your core AI work and creative explorations.

Preparing for the Ebb and Flow

The freelance journey is inherently marked by periods of feast and famine. Develop strategies to weather these fluctuations, such as prudent financial planning, cultivating passive income streams, and keeping a pipeline of prospective projects.

Contributing to the Community

Giving back to the AI community, whether through sharing knowledge, mentoring, or contributing to open-source initiatives, enriches the collective knowledge pool and can also foster personal and professional growth. These contributions can further enhance your visibility and establish you as a thought leader within the AI domain.

Conclusion

Your trajectory in AI freelancing is not merely a professional endeavor but a journey of continuous growth and contribution to the field of AI. By weaving together technical expertise, ethical practices, a commitment to lifelong learning, and active community engagement, you can forge a fulfilling and impactful career path in AI freelancing. The future is bright, and it beckons with endless possibilities—it's yours to seize and shape.

Appendices

The appendices serve as a valuable resource section, providing additional information, tools, and references to support AI freelancers in their journey. These resources are intended to complement the content covered in the preceding chapters, offering practical tools, deeper insights, and further reading options.

Appendix A: AI Tools and Software

A comprehensive list of AI tools and software that can enhance productivity, project management, and the development of AI models. This includes platforms for data analysis, machine learning libraries, AI development environments, and project management tools tailored for AI projects.

Appendix B: Online Learning Platforms and Resources

A curated selection of online platforms offering courses and tutorials in AI, machine learning, data science, and related fields. This section provides information on course offerings, specialization tracks, and certifications available to AI freelancers looking to expand their knowledge and skills.

Appendix C: Professional Networks and Communities

An overview of professional networks, online forums, and communities where AI freelancers can connect with peers, share knowledge, and find collaboration opportunities. This includes industry-specific networks, AI research groups, and social media platforms popular among AI professionals.

Appendix D: AI Conferences and Events

A calendar of notable AI conferences, workshops, and events, both virtual and in-person, that offer valuable learning and networking opportunities for AI freelancers. This section may include details on event focus areas, keynote speakers, and how to participate or submit work for presentation.

Appendix E: Ethical Guidelines and Best Practices

A guide to ethical AI development, including references to industry standards, ethical frameworks, and best practices for ensuring the responsible use of AI. This section aims to help freelancers navigate the ethical considerations inherent in AI projects.

Appendix F: Legal Templates and Resources

Sample contract templates, NDA agreements, and IP rights clauses tailored for AI freelance work. This section also includes resources for legal advice and services that specialize in tech and AI, offering freelancers a starting point for securing their work and client relationships.

Appendix G: Financial Management Tools

Recommendations for financial management tools and software designed to help freelancers manage invoicing, expenses, taxes, and budgeting. This section provides options for streamlining the financial aspects of running a freelance AI business.

Appendix H: Case Studies

A collection of case studies highlighting successful AI projects completed by freelancers. These real-world examples illustrate the application of AI solutions across various industries, showcasing the impact and value of AI freelancing work.

Appendix I: Recommended Reading

A list of essential books, articles, and research papers for AI freelancers covering topics from technical AI development to business strategies and ethical considerations in AI.

Appendix J: Glossary of AI Terms

A glossary defining key AI terms, concepts, and technologies referenced throughout the book. This resource helps ensure clarity and understanding for readers at all levels of AI expertise.

Resources for AI Freelancers

AI freelancers require a robust set of resources to navigate the complexities of the field, stay updated with the latest advancements, and manage their freelance business efficiently. Below is a compilation of essential resources across various categories to support AI freelancers in their professional journey.

Technical Tools and Libraries

- **TensorFlow**: An open-source framework for machine learning and AI developed by Google Brain.
- **PyTorch**: A deep learning library developed by Facebook's AI Research lab.
- **Scikit-learn**: A free software machine learning library for the Python programming language.
- **Keras**: An open-source software library that provides a Python interface for artificial neural networks.
- **OpenAI Gym**: A toolkit for developing and comparing reinforcement learning algorithms.

Online Learning Platforms

- **Coursera**: Offers courses in AI, machine learning, and data science from top universities and companies.
- **edX**: Provides a wide range of courses in collaboration with leading institutions, covering AI fundamentals and specialized topics.
- **Udacity**: Known for its Nanodegree programs in AI, machine learning, and related fields, offering practical, project-based learning.
- **Khan Academy**: Offers foundational courses in mathematics and computer science, essential for understanding AI algorithms.

Professional Networks and Communities

- **LinkedIn**: A professional networking platform where freelancers can connect with industry peers, join AI groups, and share insights.

- **GitHub**: Ideal for showcasing projects, collaborating on open-source initiatives, and connecting with other developers.
- **Stack Overflow**: A question-and-answer site for programmers, including a robust community of AI professionals.
- **Reddit**: Subreddits like r/MachineLearning and r/Artificial offer discussions, resources, and community support for AI enthusiasts.

Conferences and Workshops

- **NeurIPS (Conference on Neural Information Processing Systems)**: One of the largest annual AI research conferences.
- **ICML (International Conference on Machine Learning)**: A leading international academic conference in machine learning.
- **CVPR (Conference on Computer Vision and Pattern Recognition)**: A highly regarded conference in computer vision and pattern recognition.

Financial and Project Management Tools

- **FreshBooks**: Cloud-based accounting software designed for freelancers and small business owners.
- **Toggl**: A time tracking app that helps freelancers manage their work hours efficiently.
- **Asana**: A project management tool that enables freelancers to organize projects, tasks, and deadlines.

Legal Resources and Templates

- **Bonsai**: Offers customizable contract templates tailored for freelancers, including features for invoicing and payments.
- **Docracy**: An open-source repository of legal contracts and other documents, freely available for use.

Ethical AI Guidelines

- **AI Now Institute**: Publishes research and reports on the social implications of artificial intelligence and offers guidelines for ethical AI development.
- **IEEE Standards Association**: Develops standards for AI and offers resources like the "Ethically Aligned Design" document to guide ethical AI practices.

Continuous Learning and News

- **ArXiv**: An open-access archive for scholarly articles in physics, mathematics, computer science, and related fields, including AI.
- **MIT Technology Review**: Provides insightful articles on the latest in technology and AI advancements.

Freelancer Platforms

- **Upwork**: A platform connecting freelancers with clients across various fields, including AI and data science.
- **Toptal**: An exclusive network of top freelance software developers, designers, finance experts, and project managers, including AI specialists.

These resources provide a foundation for AI freelancers to enhance their technical skills, connect with the professional community, manage their freelance business, and stay informed about the latest trends and ethical considerations in AI.

Glossary of AI Terms

This glossary provides definitions for key terms and concepts related to artificial intelligence that AI freelancers might encounter in their work. Understanding these terms is crucial for effective communication with clients and peers in the field.

- **Artificial Intelligence (AI)**: The simulation of human intelligence processes by machines, especially computer systems. These processes include learning, reasoning, and self-correction.
- **Machine Learning (ML)**: A subset of AI that provides systems the ability to automatically learn and improve from experience without being explicitly programmed.
- **Deep Learning**: A subset of machine learning involving neural networks with many layers. Deep learning is used for tasks like image recognition, speech recognition, and natural language processing.
- **Neural Network**: A series of algorithms that mimic the operations of a human brain to recognize relationships between vast amounts of data. They are used in machine learning to interpret complex data inputs.
- **Natural Language Processing (NLP)**: A field of AI that focuses on the interaction between computers and humans through natural language, enabling computers

to understand, interpret, and generate human languages.

- **Computer Vision**: An AI field that trains computers to interpret and understand the visual world. Machines can accurately identify and classify objects — and then react to what they "see" — using digital images from cameras, videos, and deep learning models.
- **Reinforcement Learning**: An area of machine learning concerned with how software agents ought to take actions in an environment to maximize some notion of cumulative reward.
- **Generative Adversarial Networks (GANs)**: A class of machine learning frameworks designed by opposing networks, one generating candidates and the other evaluating them, which is useful in unsupervised learning tasks like generating realistic images or videos.
- **Algorithm**: A set of rules or instructions given to an AI program to help it learn on its own. In AI, algorithms are used to process data, learn from it, and make decisions or predictions based on the input data.
- **Data Mining**: The process of discovering patterns and knowledge from large amounts of data. The data sources can include databases, data warehouses, the Internet, and other data repositories.
- **Bias**: In AI, bias is the tendency of an algorithm to systematically favor certain outcomes due to erroneous assumptions in the machine learning process.
- **Ethical AI**: Refers to the practice of designing, developing, and deploying AI with good intention to empower employees and businesses, and fairly impact

customers and society, allowing for equity and fairness in human and machine interactions.

- **Explainable AI (XAI)**: AI in which the results of the solution can be understood by humans. It contrasts with the concept of the "black box" in machine learning where even its designers cannot explain why the AI arrived at a specific decision.
- **Quantum AI**: The use of quantum computing for computation of machine learning algorithms. Due to the nature of quantum computation, quantum AI can potentially perform more complex calculations at a faster rate than classical computers.

This glossary is not exhaustive but covers foundational terms that AI freelancers will frequently encounter. A solid grasp of these concepts is essential for effective communication and successful project delivery in the AI field.

About the Author: Ernie Braveboy

Ernie Braveboy is a renowned author who has made significant contributions to the fields of business and personal finance through his extensive array of published works. With a career dedicated to demystifying the complexities of entrepreneurship and financial management, Braveboy has established himself as a trusted voice for readers seeking practical advice and actionable strategies to navigate the economic landscape.

Core Themes in Braveboy's Writing:

- **Entrepreneurial Insight**: Braveboy's books are rich with guidance for aspiring entrepreneurs, offering step-by-step strategies for starting, managing, and scaling successful ventures in a variety of industries.
- **Financial Empowerment**: He places a strong emphasis on personal finance, covering essential topics such as budgeting, saving, investing, and wealth creation, all aimed at fostering financial independence and security.
- **Innovative Business Practices**: A consistent theme across Braveboy's work is the role of innovation in business success. He explores how embracing new technologies and innovative business models can drive growth and competitiveness.
- **Motivational Undertones**: Beyond practical advice, Braveboy's writing often touches on the importance of mindset, motivation, and resilience, underscoring the

psychological aspects of achieving business and financial success.

Writing Style and Approach:

Braveboy's writing is characterized by its accessibility and relatability. He has a talent for breaking down complex concepts into digestible, engaging content, often supplemented with real-life examples and case studies that bring his teachings to life. This approach has made his books invaluable resources for both novices and seasoned professionals alike.

Influence and Impact:

Through his insightful and inspiring books, Ernie Braveboy has cultivated a wide and diverse readership. Entrepreneurs, business professionals, and individuals looking to enhance their financial literacy have found value in his work, leading to a significant impact on many lives. Braveboy's contributions continue to inspire readers to pursue their entrepreneurial aspirations and take control of their financial destinies.

Ernie Braveboy remains a pivotal figure in the world of business and finance literature, with his works serving as essential reading for anyone looking to understand the intricacies of money management and the thrill of entrepreneurship.

Index

Conclusion

As we draw this guide to a close, I sincerely hope that it has served as a valuable resource in your journey as an AI freelancer. The dynamic world of artificial intelligence offers a landscape rich with opportunities for innovation, growth, and meaningful contributions across various industries. My aim has been to provide you with the insights, strategies, and tools necessary to navigate this exciting field successfully, enabling you to harness the potential of AI to enhance your freelance career.

Your feedback is incredibly important, not only to me but also to fellow readers who are on a similar path. If this book has helped you in any way, I kindly ask that you consider leaving a review on Amazon. Your thoughts, experiences, and reflections can guide improvements for future editions and assist others in making informed decisions about their AI freelancing endeavors.

Thank you for embarking on this journey through the pages of this guide. I wish you all the best in your AI freelance career and look forward to hearing about the incredible projects, innovations, and successes that lie ahead for you in the ever-evolving world of artificial intelligence.

THE GPT-4
ADVANTAGE
UNLOCKING THE SECRETS
OF AI-DRIVEN INCOME
ERNIE BRAVEBOY

In the groundbreaking book, "The GPT-4 Advantage: Unlocking the Secrets of AI-Driven Income," readers are invited on an enlightening journey into the world of advanced artificial intelligence and its transformative impact on generating income in the digital age. This comprehensive guide demystifies the capabilities of GPT-4, the latest iteration of the Generative Pre-trained Transformer models, and provides practical insights into leveraging this powerful AI technology for financial gain.

Inside the Book:

- **Understanding GPT-4**: Delve into the mechanics of GPT-4 and its advancements over previous models. Learn how its sophisticated natural language processing capabilities can be harnessed across various industries.
- **AI-Driven Business Opportunities**: Explore a plethora of business models and ventures that have been revolutionized by GPT-4, from content creation and digital marketing to software development and customer service enhancements.
- **Step-by-Step Guides**: Benefit from detailed tutorials and case studies that illustrate how to integrate GPT-4 into your business strategies, streamline operations, and create new avenues for income.
- **Ethical Considerations**: Navigate the ethical landscape of using advanced AI in business, ensuring responsible and sustainable practices that align with industry standards and societal expectations.

- **Future Outlook**: Gain insights into the future trajectories of AI in the business world, preparing you for upcoming trends and ensuring long-term success in an AI-driven economy.

"The GPT-4 Advantage: Unlocking the Secrets of AI-Driven Income" is not just a book; it's your roadmap to understanding and capitalizing on one of the most significant technological advancements of our time. Whether you're an entrepreneur, a freelancer, or an innovator looking to explore the potential of AI, this book offers the knowledge and tools you need to thrive in the burgeoning AI economy.

Get Your Copy Today

Dive into the world of AI-driven income with "The GPT-4 Advantage." Discover how GPT-4 can revolutionize your approach to business and income generation. Click here to explore the book on Amazon and embark on your journey to harnessing the power of advanced AI.

For more insights, updates, and access to a wealth of resources tailored to navigating the AI landscape and beyond, I warmly invite you to follow my author page. By staying connected, you'll be the first to know about new releases, deep dives into AI topics, and other valuable content designed to support your journey in the ever-evolving world of technology and freelancing.

Follow Ernie Braveboy's Author Page on Amazon to stay informed and inspired.

Thank you for your support and engagement. Together, let's explore the frontiers of AI and unlock new opportunities for innovation and growth.

www.ingramcontent.com/pod-product-compliance
Lightning Source LLC
Chambersburg PA
CBHW070124260726
48658CB00001B/256